Money and Your Church

OTHER BOOKS BY THE AUTHOR

Accounting Methods for the Small Church
Making It on a Pastor's Pay
Money Management for Ministers
Tax Planning for the Clergyman

Money and Your Church

HOW TO RAISE MORE
HOW TO MANAGE IT BETTER

Manfred Holck, Jr.

Keats Publishing, Inc.  New Canaan, Connecticut

The quotation on page 66 from *Stewards Appointed* by Dr. Raymond Olson is reprinted by permission of the Augsburg Publishing House, Minneapolis, Minnesota (copyright © 1960).

The outline of auditing procedures, pages 138-141, is from *The Auditor* by Wayne Pfundstein and reprinted by permission of the Pacific Southwest Synod of the Lutheran Church in America, Los Angeles, California (copyright © 1965).

The order for the commissioning of visitors for the Every Member Response on pages 87-89 is used with the permission of the Commission on Stewardship, Lutheran Church in America, New York.

MONEY AND YOUR CHURCH

Published in 1974 by Keats Publishing, Inc.

ISBN: 0-87983-080-8

Library of Congress Catalog Card Number: 74-75979

Printed in the United States of America

Keats Publishing, Inc.
212 Elm Street
New Canaan, Connecticut 06840

To my wife
LOIS
and our children
whose love, devotion, and sacrifice
have sustained our family's commitment
to go beyond the tithe.

CONTENTS

1. THE CHURCH'S MONEY AND WHAT IT IS ALL ABOUT 9

2. WHERE ALL THAT MONEY COMES FROM 20

3. TO TITHE OR NOT TO TITHE 42

4. HOW TO FIND MORE MONEY FOR YOUR CHURCH 59

5. WHERE ALL THE MONEY GOES (BUDGETS) 91

6. TELLING IT LIKE IT IS (RECORD KEEPING) 111

7. MAKING MONEY BY SPENDING LESS 142

8. HOW TO PAY YOUR PASTOR MORE AND BALANCE THE BUDGET, TOO 165

BIBLIOGRAPHY 185

CHAPTER ONE

The Church's Money and What It Is All About

The love of money may be the root of all evil, but not money. In fact, money, in and of itself is really nothing. It may be some pieces of paper or a few coins, in themselves of little value actually. Money may even be shells or teeth or skins or knives or guns or flour or beans. Then it might be useful for something and even of value in and of itself.

But money, as we know it, is simply pieces of paper and coins that serve as a medium of exchange, a tool we use to barter, exchange, trade and buy goods. It represents that which we have earned by our activity, or the exchange of goods. By itself it is nothing. It is not evil. On the contrary, it is obviously quite useful, no less to the church than to anyone else.

For churches, along with their pastors, would be hard pressed to do without money. Imagine a Sunday morning offering, for example, of bales of hay or stalks of corn or bleating sheep. True, offerings other than cash were made in earlier days. Today, the normal offering is cash. An offering plate full of cash is even preferable to one full of stock certificates, for the latter create some handling problems just as hay and corn and sheep do. Dollar bills and quarters are much easier to deal with. Cash money *is* useful to churches. At least it is a convenient way to take up the Sunday offering.

As an aside, here at the very beginning, there are even better ways to take up the offering than using money. In fact, if everyone would use credit cards once a month instead of money and thus charge their offerings, taking the collection could be simplified, and money—the dollars and quarters and nickels and dimes and pennies—could be eliminated. Another way is a regular transfer from one's bank account to the church's bank account. If every member did this, the rattle of paper and the clink of coins in the offering plates would be eliminated. This method would immediately create a surge of unemployment among Sunday morning church tellers. But it would work. The church would get the needed money, perhaps even more and more regularly because the offering would not depend on church attendance. Obviously there are more convenient and efficient ways of taking up the Sunday offering than simply passing the collection plates down the pews.

But cash money is still a convenient and traditional medium of exchange for the gifts of the faithful on a Sunday morning. And in the process, I believe, it also offers an important symbolic act of worship (as discussed at the end of Chapter 2). For the offering is not, or should not be, an expression of appreciation according to the worth of the service that day. Though the offering is often received immediately after the sermon in many of our worship services, it is not intended to be a response to the sermon of the day. In a former century it may have been. Even so, from the looks of some offerings on an occasional summer Sunday morning when my own efforts are less than enthusiastic, the response of the parishioners seems to match my lack of enthusiasm; I suspect that I am being paid for the worth of my sermon.

Be that as it may, money, the coins and dollar bills we all use, are useful to the church and are a significant part of the Christian worship experience besides. If for no other reasons than these, money is not evil. It is useful to the church and is an expression of commitment by the faithful.

Money is useful to the church far beyond all that, obviously. Without it, the church could hardly exist, at least not in the forms we know today. The more money the church can manage to receive, the more effectively—presumably, although not necessarily so—can it minister to the needs and concerns of those who depend upon it for spiritual sustenance. It also provides physical sustenance to its employees and the needy and anyone to whom the church makes payment with its money.

The more money the church is able to accumulate and use, the more significant will be its impact upon people, upon the society within which it exists. Thus, as I see it, money in the church is certainly not evil. Rather, it is useful, important and necessary for the survival of the church itself.

As with anything important, though, the very usefulness of money to the church requires a stewardship, a management and a husbandry of exceptional vigor.

Obviously the church obtains money by means other than just the offering on a Sunday morning, or any of the gifts it receives. The church can increase its money supply by better spending procedures, more efficient management of resources and careful control of the spending process. That is why it is possible for one church—because of careful spending, conservation and control—to have more money than another church that handles its money supply in an unorganized and slipshod way, not taking management of money seriously.

Too often the cry of a church for more money is only a hidden admission of poor, inept and stupid management of the resources already on hand. Less cry and a more organized approach to money management in many congregations may be a far better stewardship of these resources. It could conceivably resolve an impending overdrawn bank account quite nicely.

I see money management in the church as a process of resource allocation through carefully planned and controlled procedures for securing, spending, conserving and saving money. In other words, church money management and procurement includes fund raising primarily, but it also includes the purchasing of goods and services—including the payment of benevolence commitments—and the saving of money or earning more of it through investments and careful cash flow management.

And that is what this book is all about. Briefly these are the matters that I will be discussing.

First of all, what are some of the more obvious ways of raising money efficiently and effectively? I suggest the obvious as still being the most important and efficient, the Sunday morning offering. That act of giving alone, it seems to me, serves as a significant expression of the membership's interest in and dedication to the program of the church. Yet if that response is only a response to the needs of the church for more money, it is a selfish response.

The only legitimate offering is one of sacrifice in response to the love of God. Despite the need of the church for money, if there is not this self-giving response, of what value, except selfish pride, is the gift? The church could do just as well, probably better, to join in with the United Appeals Fund if the membership's motive for giving is no more than to meet a need, real or imagined.

All of which suggests that there is a real responsibility among the membership and its leaders to inspire a response of outflowing, generous grateful hearts. Then the coffers will overflow. For church giving must be motivated by more than just some desperate financial need. It must come in response to God's love. Of course, once the gift is made, then certainly the financial needs can be met. And perhaps sometimes needs must be emphasized to get the dollars required to put on a new roof or build an addition or replace the parking lot. But if the church constantly pleads for more money on any other basis than God's love for his children, it may as well join ranks with the YWCA or Rotary or the Salvation Army.

Fund raising is a primary responsibility of the members of the church. Without it the local church could not exist. But its motivation must be Christ-centered. And then, from there, it will generate the substantial inflow of money required to keep the church going in that community where it is supposed to serve.

Church funds come from other places besides the offering, of course. Indeed, the last wills of many of the faithful make large and handsome gifts to the church through bequests. The accumulations of these generosities over the years are the main sustenance for many churches, especially today. Don't knock the possibilities and don't ignore them either. Your members can quite appropriately be encouraged to remember the work of their church in their wills.

I believe, however, that the sales of goods and services in far too many congregations is another matter. It seems to me that such activity often occupies excessive hours of baking pies and cakes and catering dinners to the detriment of real service to the church. Hourly rates of 30 and 40 cents are not uncommon considering the return on such questionable business activities—often in competition with the local bakery and restaurant besides. Yet, as questionable as bake sales and dinners may be, though often justified because of the fellowship created by sweating over a hot stove together, many church boards still anticipate with glee the annual contribution of the women's society to the budget of the church.

I submit that there must be better ways of raising money in the name of fellowship. At least I will more readily contribute my $10 in cash to help buy a new piano than volunteer to run the basketball shoot at my church's carnival for that same purpose. But for all too many churches, profits from the annual bazaar and the turkey dinner are the difference between bankruptcy and just hanging on. So they hang on, too often without really knowing why, certainly without realizing that there may be a better and more useful way, certainly a more "Christian" way, to raise funds for their church.

A church can raise its money in many ways. For example, insurance policies offer an opportunity for members to give money on their death, but pay for it while they live. More important, the designation of a church as beneficiary or owner of a policy assures some continuity in the giving commitment of especially generous donors. Haven't you known of congregations in which the loss of one family's giving on account of death has played havoc with that congregation's budget for a long, long time? The assignment of insurance is an important way to bridge that gap, besides making possible larger sums of money than would otherwise have been available.

An aggressive deferred charitable giving program offers

financial security down the road, too. The giving of money now, contingent on an annuity for life, at least offers a certainty of half that gift at the donor's death, maybe more. And it may offer a more enjoyable choice to the donor than even a bequest. For that donor might just live to see his gift put to the purpose for which it was given; that is, assuming the congregation can fund the annuity and still provide the service or facility donated.

The careful use of idle money through short term investments offers another choice in making more money for the church. Offerings come in peaks. Any minister knows that—at Christmas and Easter. Expenses tend to run evenly month by month. Excessive cash balances in January and April can be a significant source of more money through brief, interim investments.

No doubt, the innovative lay leader or pastor can find other ways to raise more money for the church. He need only remember that the church must not compromise its objectives nor flaunt its purpose for being, just for the sake of a few more dollars. He can find many acceptable ways to improve the flow of dollars into the coffers of his church.

But simply getting more money is not the only way to have more of it. Resource allocation, the wise use of what you already have, intelligent management of spending and conserving and saving of money are extremely important, too.

So, in the second place, the way a church spends its money makes a tremendous difference in the way it can later allocate its remaining resources. You simply cannot expect a church to be particularly stable financially if it spends willy-nilly, reacting to every crisis and plea without a priority listing of allocations or a plan of spending. Leave all spending decisions to the whim of the pastor or a key lay leader, and it's not surprising to find the finances of a church in a state of utter confusion. A church can spend money without a budget, to be sure, a lot of money, but it will probably be disastrous spending. A budget will not guarantee financial stability, of course, but at least it may be a warning of impending doom long before the inevitable occurs.

More than that, a budget is a plan for spending, an agreed-upon, way-in-advance program of how the monies of the church will be spent. It is authorization for spending, providing funds are available to be spent, of course. It is a guide, a tool, a plan for spending. And it offers an opportunity to control that spending.

Proper controls on spending can effectively stretch a church's budget. It is true that a strong but understanding hand on the bank account of the church may create frustrations for the liberals and social activists. But I believe it can expand the overall success of the missions of the church. This is not dictatorial control, but management of resources with a plan in mind and a knowledge of funds available and anticipated.

A budget, control and a system or plan for spending go hand in hand. So proper procedures for buying, ordering, receiving merchandise and invoicing are also important for keeping money in the bank. If everyone and his friend is authorized to buy paper clips, you will have paper clips left over when the church is long gone. Unless some kind of system—purchase requisitions and the like—is set up, you will be forever throwing money down the drain. It's inevitable. Money management, and thus the preservation of money, requires a plan and a procedure. Put some teeth into it and you've got control. The actual survival of the church may very well depend upon someone saying "no" occasionally.

Further, unless you know how the money is being spent, you will not be able to measure the success of the plan for spending. An accounting system is essential if you want to know how much the plan for spending has stretched the dollars that can be spent. You will also find out, rather quickly, with a good record keeping system, how much you have spent and what is left to last until the Easter and Christmas crowds come through again.

Then, in the third place, endowment funds offer an opportunity for more money for your church. Now not very many congregations have endowment funds or any surplus funds to invest. Every dime given is usually spent twice over. But sometimes, through whatever source—a bequest, the sale of property, judicious accumulation of funds—an endowment fund of sorts is available. Then, if the church is to avoid the slow but inevitable dissipation of the accumulation, it must develop plans to conserve and to protect that money.

And, as is supposed to happen with a well-managed endowment fund, there will in fact then be more money for the church. But it never just happens.

There must be a plan with objectives and goals and procedures. Investment counsel must be secured, which normally means finding someone entirely unrelated to the church and unemotionally involved. Professional investment counsel is important, no matter the cost of the service or the size of the endowment. The facts show that successful funds are managed by professionals. Lackluster or disastrous funds are often at the mercy of some inept but well-intentioned member who owns a few shares of AT&T and calls himself an investment analyst.

But more money can be raised for the church with the income from endowment funds. So, an active campaign for capital gifts or bequests is a legitimate goal for better church resource allocation, providing these monies are subsequently managed well.

In addition, a church can indeed save money or make more money, whichever way you want to put it, by careful management of its spending. Conserving the funds you have is as important as raising more or spending less.

For example, good cash management requires taking every available discount as late as possible, but taking it for sure. Do you? Two percent, 10 days, net 30, can mean a $2 savings on a $100 purchase. Over the months and through many invoices, that adds up. The church that misses its discounts is simply spending more money than it should.

Put together a cash flow schedule and you can plot your cash needs and make money, too. Along with short term investments during peak offerings, this will help cut interest costs during the summer drought. Paying premiums annually, avoiding finance charges and finding ways to do without every new piece of office equipment persistent salesmen try to foist upon unsuspecting secretaries: all will help to conserve the funds of the church.

Also, a church can avoid paying almost any tax, including property, sales, income, payroll and unemployment taxes. Of course, there may be reasons why you will elect to pay a tax. For example, you may pay payroll taxes so church employees can be covered by Social Security. But you don't have to pay most taxes. Wherever available, exemptions for property tax ought to be requested, whether on the church house or parsonage.

I believe that more money for your church is really the process of efficient resource allocation and good management of what you have, which is all more than simply raising more money, although that is a principal objective. Making money for your church is also the process of good spending habits, good investment techniques and careful cash management, which of course is what this book is really all about.

There is simply no pot of gold at the end of the rainbow to fill a shrinking church treasury. And persistent gouging of the membership to cough up yet another $10 bill gets old all too soon. You can get more money for your church by lifting the sights of your members to give more, to be sure, but with techniques that do not offend. You can also get more money for your church by managing your resources well and paying attention to such little things as where all the postage stamps and paper clips go. Giving attention to the larger matters—the pastor's compensation, the heat bill, benevolence commitments, lawn care—may make a significant difference, too, in the balance in the bank at the end of the year. Fund raising and management of available resources go hand in hand toward making more money available to your church.

Like it or not, money is the essence of your church's survival. You need it. So you cannot ignore money as though your church and its program can go on perpetually no matter what. Faith is not a belief in the assurance of constant financial viability. God does provide, of course. But in a society where goods and services are bought and sold competitively with money, even the church must appreciate the value of the dollar if it expects to carry its program to the community—a community, incidentally, which desperately needs what the church can provide for it, including its money.

I am convinced that there is always more money for your church somewhere. But it just doesn't always come running when you want it. Most often you have to go out looking for it. In fact, an aggressive plan of fund raising and of conservation may be the only thing that will keep your church from going under next year. Indeed, a good plan for resource allocation could be the very key to the survival of your church.

Money is not evil. In fact, it is really good. In the church, it gets the work of the Lord done in a way that would be impossible without it. His kingdom depends on it and his church cannot survive without it.

CHAPTER TWO

Where All That Money Comes From

	UNITED STATES CHURCHES	CANADIAN CHURCHES
Total Bodies	39	21
Full or Confirmed Membership	41,848,229	2,202,285
Total Contributions	$4,615,607,162	$189,789,810
Per Capita	110.29	86.18
Congregational Finances	3,690,816,749	142,781,584
Per Capita	88.20	64.83
Benevolences	924,790,413	47,008,226
Per Capita	22.09	21.35
Benevolence as a Percentage of Total Contributions	20.0 percent	24.8 percent

Source: NCC 1973 Church Financial Statistics for 1972

Giving, by people, to churches, is still the single largest source of funds for the local congregation—almost 5 billion dollars in 1972 alone! And the future of the church in this country depends on that support continuing in an ever-increasing proportion.

Unlike state supported churches in other countries, the church in North America is supported entirely by the giving of its members and other interested persons. The Sunday morning offering is the source of funds every church must depend upon if it is to survive. Thus the emphasis put on that simple act, the incentives created to sustain and enlarge that response, even the gimmicks foisted upon an otherwise unsuspecting congregation to raise more money, all generally center right there on a Sunday morning in the offering plates. If for no other reason than that, that the very existence of the church depends upon it, the offering is one of the most significant acts of worship in the Christian church.

In Chapter four of this book, a program of fund raising for the local congregation is outlined. In subsequent chapters, other ways to get more money for your church are explained. The purpose of this chapter is to explain the various sources from which churches can receive funds in addition to the obvious Sunday offering. I will offer suggestions on how to go about getting more money from several of these other sources.

But just to emphasize the significance of that weekly Sunday ritual, compare these statistics among the major denominations with highest per capita contributions in 1972. Where does your group and your congregation fit in?

DENOMINATION	MEMBERSHIP	TOTAL CONTRIBUTIONS	PER CAPITA
Seventh-day Adventists	449,188	$187,400,761	$417.20
Missionary Church, Inc.	20,078	7,592,012	378.13
Brethren in Christ Church	9,730	3,419,357	351.42
Free Methodist Church of North America	65,167	21,845,170	335.22

The Evangelical Church of North America	9,843	$ 2,955,473	$ 300.26
The Evangelical Covenant Church of America	69,815	18,726,259	268.23
Church of the Nazarene	404,732	97,902,429	241.89
Church of God (Anderson, Indiana)	155,920	37,131,238	238.14
Baptist General Conference	111,364	26,448,368	237.49

Calculating the potential giving for any congregation is explained in Chapter four; but by comparing statistics available from the Internal Revenue Service, actual giving as a percentage of adjusted gross income can be determined. The statistics (percentage of income contributed) are not very impressive–it's far short of a tithe–but at least for those taxpayers itemizing their contributions, it tells the percentage of income given away. The chart on the opposite page indicates the way the figures look for 1972.

Draw whatever conclusion you want from this data, but it is clear that as a percentage of income, the vast majority of people support their church with less than a full 10 percent enthusiastic commitment. Obviously, such a percentage goal has not as yet been achieved by many Christians; but there is growing evidence, as suggested by the chart above, that more people are at least giving away a larger proportion (and more dollars) of their income. (Tithing is discussed in the next chapter.)

Just consider the significance giving would gain if those percentages were 10 percent instead of 3, 4, or 5 percent. The average gift would jump substantially, often doubling, and the church, your church, would have more money than it would know how to handle at the moment. It is a delightful thought, one every church leader probably contemplates especially at the end of the year. For that's when too few dollars are being stretched to meet commitments for this year and too few pledges are being exaggerated in planning for the next year. Too bad the thought is only a dream.

% of Contributions to Adjusted Gross Income†
(Based upon IRS itemized tax returns)

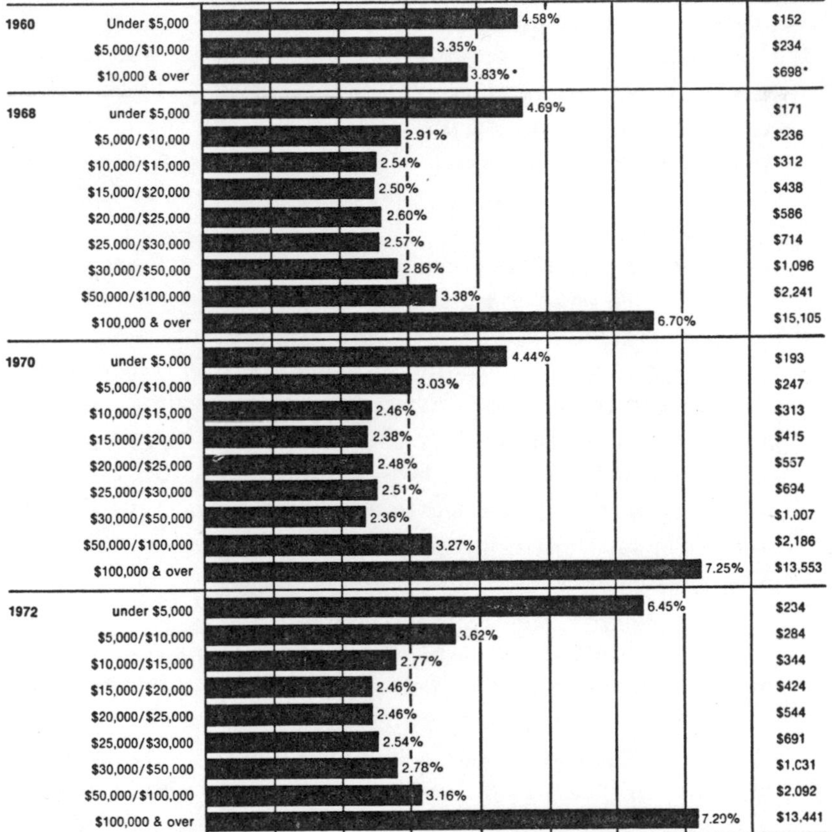

†The average amount contributed was determined by dividing those returns that itemized contributions into the total contributions figure. The adjusted gross income figure used was for all returns with itemized deductions.

**Breakdown for returns between $10,000 and $15,000 not available before 1966.*

Reprinted by permission of the American Association of Fund-Raising Counsel, Inc.

One more statistic to put giving to churches in perspective with giving to all causes. The facing chart shows how religious organizations compare with other groups as recipients of the giver's dollar.

These statistics suggest that the church has a built-in bias toward itself that consistently nets its program more dollars than any other charitable group. The church that can capitalize on that advantage will indeed be able to get more money for its programs and activities.

Giving is a very personal act, and most people do not easily change the character of their generosities. The church's advantage is obvious. Its procedure for taking the initiative in developing that advantage is not so clear. It is the purpose of this book to try to offer suggestions for improving the statistics.

There are all sorts of motives for giving. Someone could write a whole book on that. One is guilt. I suppose we could generate a greater response to church collections simply by arousing a sense of guilt among the membership. The profits, for example, that North Americans make by owning half the industries in South America and consuming 75 percent of their exported raw materials is significant. United Nations statistics show that even the gap between average per capita income in the United States and other countries is widening. Our guilt could shame us into giving more.

Fear can motivate giving, too. The energy crunch and ecological disasters resulting from our headlong rush to use up natural resources offer a foretaste of what may happen. Out of fear we can give more and use less. We can even be made to want less, to suffer more, to identify with mission and service in a way none of us may comprehend at the moment. To motivate stewardship on the basis of guilt or fear is a real possibility—and some church leaders do it, with notable success.

I would prefer to motivate with grace and forgiveness,

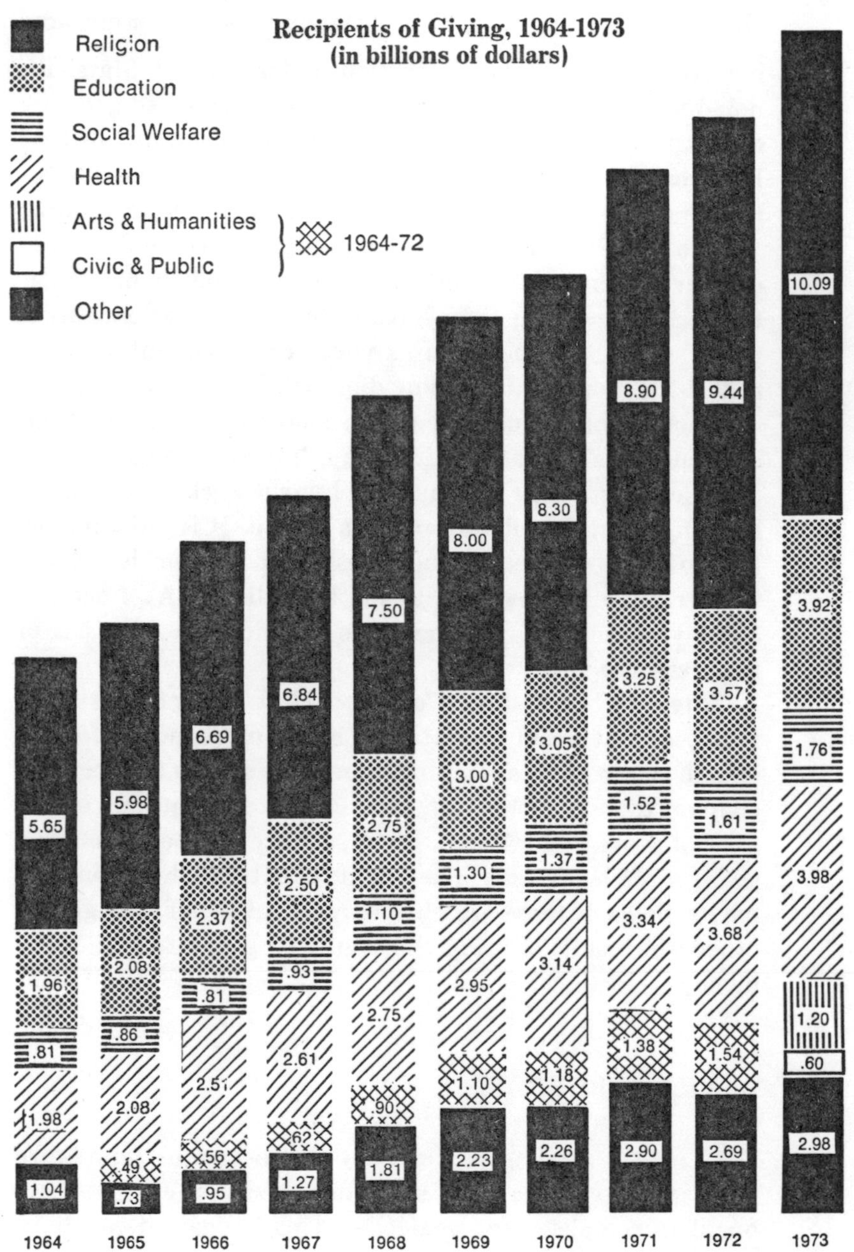

Reprinted by permission of the American Association of Fund-Raising Counsel, Inc.

however. To follow the suggestion of Dr. Robert Marshall, noted world churchman, "we would urge people to give out of gratitude and good management rather than out of law. Forgiveness makes us strong in the struggle against exploitation, and capable of reinvesting the wealth in human values."

No matter how you assess the current economic status of your own members, they are probably much better off financially now than they have ever been. Inflation affects their pocketbooks the same as yours or mine. But we dare not let the proportion of giving diminish for that reason. You may not be able to convince people that they are richer than ever and thus increase their giving, but you don't dare let them feel poor either for that one hour a week on a Sunday morning when the offering plate is passed. It is more important to help people realize their blessings and then "lead them to ever more worthy objects for their lives." At least the Sunday morning offering becomes a concrete expression of that response.

Stewardship, and thus one's total giving, includes more than just that weekly donation. There's more money for the church in other forms of giving, too. As I noted in the previous chapter, there is money for your church in bequests, in the sales of goods and services, life insurance proceeds, deferred giving plans, short term investments of extra cash and endowments. Some of these are obviously direct benefits of giving, others the results of using those gifts to generate even more money.

A WILLS PROGRAM

There is nothing particularly distinctive or impressive about making out a will. It is an act which every person ought to complete. For neglecting this obligation can have significant financial consequences as to the final disposition of one's estate. A will offers the one sure way for you to decide who gets what of all you have. It is your way of designating how your estate will be divided among your heirs and the organizations you want to support. Without a will you don't have any choice. Other people will make that distribution for you. And if you had lived to see the way it was done, you probably would not have liked what you saw.

The importance to the church of emphasizing the making of a will is in the opportunity it presents to influence bequests for its own benefit or that of other charitable groups. A will has nothing really to do with the church, but when a Christian makes out a will, then the church, it is hoped, will be part of that person's conscious plan of estate distribution.

A "Christian Will" is no more than the will of a Christian. It is neither more nor less legal than any other will. Strictly speaking, there is no such thing as a Christian Will. But a properly drawn will can surely witness to the Christian's belief and commitment. The Christian's will will testify that he believes in Jesus Christ. It will make fair and sensible distribution of assets to provide for the person's family and loved ones. It may express the maker's preference on funeral arrangements. It could specify how certain treasured keepsakes may be given to special friends. But most important, it will be an act of stewardship by providing a proportion of that estate for the work of the Lord. Any bequest, no matter the amount, will simply reflect the testator's interest and commitment to the capital and continuing needs of the church and its agencies. The Christian's will includes a stewardship commitment that makes provision for a bequest to the church.

But that kind of a response from the membership does not just happen. It must be cultivated and planned and encouraged. And the results may never be known to those who push the plan. For a wills program in the church is a low keyed, on-going educational program that has a clear objective but no real anticipation of near-term results. Bequests received today will benefit this generation, but the seed for the gift may have been made long ago by persons now long gone or unknown. The church that pushes a wills program expecting an immediate upsurge in bequests is in for a disappointment. There may be some quick results, but not likely. A wills program just goes on and on and on. And someday, significant results may begin to show. Still, I believe it is a very important way to get more money for your church.

The arguments against making a will are all familiar. Only rich people need to make out a will. But anyone who owns anything needs a will to make sure that even what he has, no matter how small, goes where he wants it to go.

That making a will means you will die sooner is another fallacy. Obviously, writing your will has nothing to do with the future state of your health. On the contrary, a will offers therapeutic value in that one feels he has done a good thing. It may even prolong life.

Some people hesitate to have a will drawn by a competent attorney because they consider the cost to be exorbitant. Well, it does cost something, but it is not necessarily excessive. In the end, it may cost more not to have had a will done professionally. An attorney familiar with the legal technicalities of the law in the state where you live, can save you and your estate untold dollars. Besides, to pay for a well-written will makes certain that any bequests for the church are drawn properly and are therefore not subject to later contest.

Procrastination is probably the main reason why people do not make a will. What's the hurry? But the hurry is precisely the urgency of making sure your estate is spread out the way you want it to be. Now is the time to make a will, even if you do expect to make it to 100. However, you just might not! A will now could save your heirs some disappointments later on.

The plan, then, for an ongoing congregational wills emphasis educational program might go something like this.

First of all, you'll need a Wills Emphasis committee (Oh, no, not another committee!) or at least someone who will push the program and try to keep the interest going. The group should include a cross section of people, among them some who know something about wills—bankers, attorneys, accountants. Such people may also serve as a professional advisory group for the wills program. The committee, of course, will not write any wills. It will only plan the program and serve as a resource to the congregation.

A program of action would suggest getting most of the following things done, sometime:

1. Distribution of special materials about wills—special mailings, bulletin inserts, take-home pieces.

2. Encouragement of wills as a program topic at regular meetings of church groups or at special meetings just for the discussion of wills.

3. Provision of assistance to church members who need or want help with their own wills.

4. Provision for regular and systematic follow-up on inquiries and periodic distribution of pertinent materials. A regular congregational-wide emphasis can be repeated about every third year. Encourage participants to review their wills frequently. Like writing letters, a will needs periodic revision because circumstances do change with time.

An effective Wills Emphasis program, of course, involves more than just writing a will. Total estate planning includes tax considerations, life insurance, capital asset distribution, personal money management and a whole host of other topics.

Specific information on bequests to the church is critical. A program of information on what such bequests can do for the Kingdom gets to the heart of the program.

The culminating effort of the committee, though, is probably a special program just to emphasize estate planning. Such programs can take on all kinds of direction and agenda, but you'll need to adapt the procedure that fits your needs and your people the best. A filmstrip or film may be helpful. There are many available. An expert on estate planning speaking from the Christian perspective can be useful. An opportunity for questions and answers is crucial. Helpful take-home materials should be distributed.

Bequests do offer an opportunity for generating more money for the church. But will-making is more than a process for building up the treasury of the church. More important, it is an opportunity to express one's Christian commitment through the stewardship of all his or her resources.

Chester A. Myron, Chairman of the Interfaith Commission on Christian Family Financial Planning, has written:

"Will-making involves a new dimension in Christian stewardship. It is a dimension already achieved by some, but not yet ventured into by many. In proportion as church members come to maturity in this realm of stewardship—the stewardship of capital in contrast with the stewardship of income—the church will be financially equipped and ready for the opportunities for Christ that lie ahead.

"Most Christians have, I think, a degree of understanding about 'Christian calling.' We recognize that God calls all men, that His own hear His voice and seek to respond to it. Response on the part of young adults may take the form of affiliating with a congregation—for the sake of their children, perhaps, but also for the joys of participating in the Christian fellowship. At times it may take the form of accepting the chairmanship of a key committee, of being named Sunday school superintendent or of serving in some other special way. We've all been mindful of a sense of call in instances like these.

"Not so readily grasped, however, is the concept that God's call is a continuing one, extending over all of life's span. God's call is not something to be experienced only by youth or by adults in the full vigor of life. God's call comes again and again—to every believer, in whatever situation he or she happens to be. It is only the response that changes—its nature, its manner, its method—but not the call.

"A spiritual insight not yet caught by most church members is the realization that in the evening years of life, when the demands and pressures of the earlier years are past, there may be opportunities to witness to one's faith in ways that simply weren't possible earlier—in other words, to respond in still another way to God's continuing call. A Wills Emphasis effort in a congregation may be the means through which many achieve a new dimension in their Christian stewardship."

Write a Letter to Your Widow

Writing a letter to your widow may sound morbid but your survivors do need to know about some things not normally included in your will. Unlike your will, this "letter of instruction" is a rather personal type of letter, addressed to your spouse, or children, or attorney, written like almost any letter is written. It is your way of telling your family just how you would like your personal affairs to be handled.

You need to have a will to start with. That's first, of course. In it, your attorney will spell out precisely what disposition is to be made of your assets. He will specify certain other conditions as well, all in proper legal terminology so there is no problem when your will is probated. It is a professional legal document administered by the courts.

You write your letter of instruction, though, in whatever language you want. It is not a legal document and no one is bound by it. But at least it tells your family what you preferred and where to look for your important papers and documents. It is the kind of letter that sets out all the important little details not normally included in your will.

The First National City Bank of New York suggests that you include these items:

1. List approximately how much cash and property your family and heirs may expect. This may include an inventory of all your property, including insurance proceeds, and who is to get what. Don't overlook Social Security and your own denominational death benefits.

2. Specify the names, addresses, and telephone numbers of persons to be notified at your death. For example: your attorney, friends, church officials, bank, insurance company and Social Security office.

3. List the location of your important papers—your will, birth and marriage certificates, insurance policies, Social Security number and other important personal papers.

4. List the account numbers of your checking and savings accounts. List all credit card account numbers. Note where your passbooks are located. Make a list of what is in your safe-deposit box, where it is located, and where the key is. Record facts about any outstanding debts you owe other people. Indicate where your income tax returns are filed.

5. Record the names of all insurance companies, telephone numbers of agents and all policy numbers. Include life, accident, car, homeowner, medical and mortgage insurance.

6. If you have securities—stocks and bonds—list them and where they are located, and their present value.

7. Add any other details that may be important. Note the location of all deeds to real estate, list properties, note

the location of tax receipts, include any facts needed that would help your spouse sell your home if necessary or sell other properties you own.

8. Write out any special wishes that you have, or personal desires—where you want your children to go to college, if you want your body or organs used for medical research, what kind of funeral you would prefer (your survivors, however, should have the freedom to decide what will help them out most), which options you prefer your wife to take on your insurance proceeds, etc.

Then send a copy of your letter to your lawyer or executor, put one with your will, and keep one copy at home where your family can find it quickly. Be sure that your letter can be easily understood by anyone who reads it. Your spouse may have died with you in an accident. Date your letter.

And then, by all means, keep your letter updated and the information current. Once a year, at least, go back through the letter and change it as necessary. You will do well to do the same with your will.

GIVING THROUGH LIFE INSURANCE

Estate planning also includes the disposition of insurance policies. Most churchgoers carry some kind of life insurance. As they grow older, those policies are needed less desperately than when family responsibilities are more significant. But those same policies offer an excellent opportunity for members, especially those of modest means, to give substantial sums.

As you work with your congregation, you may want to encourage such gifts. They are a natural part of any long-range giving program. Those who respond to this plan of giving will not only enjoy an immediate income-tax deduction but will also have the satisfaction of making a more substantial gift than they otherwise could have made.

A life insurance gift is a "for sure" gift. At death your church will get the full amount of the policy without delay, probate or contest. Furthermore, your church is sure of getting the full amount from the policyholder. It cannot be reduced by anyone. An insurance policy is certainly an easy personal way to give. It is economical, or at least can be, depending on total premium payments. It is obviously a convenient way to give. And with the help of a competent underwriter, almost any convenient arrangement can be worked out.

An insurance underwriter can advise your membership on the best way to give life insurance to your church. It may be done by naming the church co-beneficiary of a policy, for example. You could encourage members simply to take out a new policy for the benefit of your church. In fact, you could organize a program in your church through which every member is encouraged to take out a $1,000 policy on his life naming the church the beneficiary. The member pays the premium and takes an annual tax deduction as long as he keeps up the payments. If he stops paying the premium, the church can take the cash value or a paid-up policy for the designated amount, or take up payment of the premium itself.

Maybe you will want to encourage your members to assign their policy dividends to the church. These would be a tax deduction also. When members make large pledges to your church, they may wish to take out policies covering any bequests they have promised to your church, just to make sure the church gets the money. Those members who are no longer insurable can take out a policy on the life of someone else, name the church the beneficiary, pay the premiums and get a tax deduction to boot.

Remember that if your members name the church as the irrevocable beneficiary of an existing policy or take out a new policy for the church, they can take a tax deduction for the premium they pay as though they were contributing the amount to the church. Or if they give the church a policy they already own, they can deduct the cash value as a contribution plus any premiums they continue to pay.

DEFERRED GIVING-WHILE-LIVING

There are, of course, other ways in which members can give substantial sums to the church without waiting for their wills to be probated. They can actually give while they live through the use of any one of several other deferred giving plans. Known by several names, such plans are referred to as gift annuities, life income contracts, charitable remainder trusts. The technicalities of such plans are not important for the purposes of this discussion (a competent attorney can explain the legalities). The idea, however, is an increasingly important concept in discussions on estate planning and giving to the church.

Essentially these plans offer the donor an opportunity to give a gift of securities or real estate or other property while alive, subject to some kind of periodic payment to the donor for life or a specified period of time. The gift itself therefore is subject to providing that income payment and cannot be dissipated until the conditions of the gift are finally met.

This kind of gift offers a unique opportunity. The donor can give a large sum now without seriously jeopardizing his personal resources. He can know then that the gift, deferred as it may be, will, nevertheless, one day be used for the purposes designated by him, the donor.

Thus, a person can give $10,000 subject to an annuity for life. The annuity payments will presumably be made first from the income generated by that gift, secondly out of the principal itself. Insurance rates are generally standardized throughout the charitable giving "industry" with the expectation that for even the longest life at least one-half of the original principal will remain. More often the remainder is much more.

Or, instead of a return of principal, the donor may be guaranteed only the income generated by the gift. At death the full principal gift, therefore, is still available for use in carrying out the donor's original intentions.

There are variations on these programs. As government tax rules change, the manner in which these kinds of gifts may be made also changes. Thus anyone anticipating such a gift needs the advice of a competent tax attorney or accountant for preparing the necessary documents.

Deferred gifts can be an important source of funds for any church willing to develop a promotional program. It truly offers a unique opportunity to get more money for your church over the long term. Write to your denominational offices. They will be glad to offer specific help to your congregation for developing such a program.

Deferred giving programs, rather than interfering with the current giving to your church, tend to increase regular giving. As the vision of what can be done through greater giving catches on, it spills over into current giving as well as long-term giving.

OTHER SOURCES OF FUNDS

Endowment funds offer an important source of additional money for your church. Not many churches have significant funds in this category, but those that do, manage to support many worthwhile programs with them.

Obviously you will not be considering this type of source for more money unless you have some kind of fund ready to use in this way. Most often endowment funds are created when some member suddenly leaves a substantial sum to the church through a will. Then there is a decision to be made on what to do with that $10,000 or $20,000. An endowment fund will at least generate an ongoing flow of dollars through income if that is where the bequest is put. Otherwise, it would finance some much needed capital improvement now. Then there would be no further income, at least not in the usual sense of dividends or interest.

Endowment funds can be encouraged simply through normal fund raising activities. If an endowment fund is what you want instead of a building, you can ask people for gifts to that purpose. Or, as bequests may be received, the church policy can direct that such funds be placed in an endowment fund, only the income to be used for the program. Or the bequests may specify investment in an endowment fund.

Endowment fund management is important. Competent counsel is crucial. Disposition of unrestricted income may well be determined by a committee of the church, but management of the fund, the generation of that income and investment of the principal must be left to professionals outside the church. To do otherwise only courts disaster. Ask an attorney for advice in getting started.

The investment of idle cash offers a good opportunity for more money, especially for larger congregations. Idle cash? What's that? What church ever has money just lying around not being used? Well, many churches actually do. And that is because offerings are not normally received on a consistent, regular, monthly basis. Offerings are seasonal. At Christmas and Easter they are far more than you need. In the summer they are never enough. So, when those fluctuations are significant, it is important to put the extra, unneeded cash of

Christmas and Easter to work in order to make up for the cost of borrowing money in the summer.

Practically, though, few churches really ever have the large sums of cash required to make an idle-cash investment program work. A typical savings and loan account would offer some benefit for at least three months at a time. Larger certificates of deposit in the same places for a longer timespan generate a higher rate of return. In multiples of $100,000 and for any length of time, as much as $25 a day can be earned through the purchase of Treasury bills, and certain other certificates of deposit at your local bank.

The point is that idle cash sitting in a checking account is not doing the church any good at all. In fact, it is costing the church money. It ought to be invested, if possible, and thus be generating some more money for the church. And even the "float" (checks written but not yet clearing the bank) in that checking account can work for the church, too. Your treasurer is the key to a successful short term investment program. He should be aggressively finding ways to keep the idle cash of the church at work.

There are those congregations that raise significant sums of money by selling goods and services. It is of course a way to raise more money for the church, but its motivations, pressures and excesses often seem to me to run counter to the traditions of the church, especially the church's emphasis on free-will giving. Yet turkey dinners, bazaars and similar festivities do offer an important opportunity for fellowship. They provide a good way to do things together as a church for a common purpose—more money in the till.

It is not the purpose of this chapter to defend or encourage such practices. Nor is there any point in describing all the different ways a church can raise money through such activity. It is evident that congregations do so, and those who consider that avenue a justifiable way to get more money out of the membership (and friends) will dream up amply successful schemes. It is a way to get more money for the church, but is it a desirable way to encourage proper stewardship attitudes and responses to the great gifts God has given us?

WHAT'S IN AN OFFERING ANYWAY?*

"What'll we do while we pass the collection plates?" The question, posed by a teenager preparing a worship service, brings a smile to the lips and a tear to the eye. For the youngster has his finger on a real problem: the offering is the most neglected, and yet one of the most important, parts of liturgy.

Could there be any connection between deficiency in stewardship and the insignificance we delegate to the offering? Maybe we need some interpretation.

In the first place, we are offering, not collecting. God's grace coming to us through the Word and Sacraments initiates our response: an offering inspired by love, not appeasement or obligation. Christians recognize this as sacrifice. That is, self-giving on the part of the congregation in response to the sacrament, which is self-giving on the part of God.

Secondly, God performs miracles with our offerings. In response to hearing our commission through the Word and in preparation for the Eucharistic meal, we give money, bread and wine. And God takes these very human gifts and uses them for his holy purpose. They become vehicles of his grace!

Our money supports and expands the ministry of the church, and our bread and wine convey the body and blood of the Lord. What we surrender to him becomes the means

*Reprinted from the Florida Synod Newsletter. Used with permission. Written by Gretchen Marz.

for receiving him! As Christ came in common flesh to complete the uncommon task of the world's redemption—so our common gifts, when offered in faith and love to God, become fit for the uncommon task of administering his means of grace.

Finally, we should see offering as our commitment to mission. It is a put-our-money-where-our-mouth-is situation. Not only our money, but our life with its precious time and individual talents. God gave us all; he expects all in return. Neither money, nor abilities nor time can stand alone as a full offering. This goes for clergy and laity alike.

Liturgy means "the work or action of the people." In no part of the liturgy is the "people's work" more evident than in their offerings to God. Naturally, the more clergy-oriented a service is, the more neglected the offering of the laity. So, the first rule-of-thumb should be—let the people in on the action.

Some suggestions:

—Have an offering procession. One member of each family presents the family's gift at the altar.

—Sing songs of dedication during the procession. (Preferably not the doxology, which is a song of praise and best suited to an entrance hymn rather than offertory.)

—Prepare laymen to offer prayers from their places in the congregation.

—Receive covenant notes written by people who wish to promise additional time, dedicate their talents, etc.

—Receive gifts of foodstuffs, cleaning materials, books, clothing for world relief, etc., in your offerings.

—Have a different family each week serve as hosts (ushers). They would greet the worshippers, pass the offering plates, provide the bread and wine and bring the offering forward in behalf of the congregation.

—Report finances in terms of work accomplished rather than in dollars and cents.

When a person sees himself as being presented on that offering plate–his time, her abilities, their money . . . when a person begins to grasp the miracles performed by God with our very human offerings . . . then that person will comprehend the mystery of "It is more blessed to give than to receive."

CHAPTER THREE

To Tithe or Not to Tithe

There is more money for your church in offerings that are tithes or more.

Let's talk about giving. After all, that is the heart of any fund raising program carried on by the church. All the other sources of funds pale to insignificance, usually, in the face of the overwhelming support that does (and must) come from the voluntary, free-will giving of the membership. Without it the church in America would cease to exist (contrary to the tax-supported state churches in Europe). So this subject of giving is a crucially important topic. It is also kind of primary to the purpose of this book. So, let's do talk about giving.

Is giving really necessary? To some people that is a primary question. To others, the thought has never occurred.

For some people, especially those outside the church or who are at most lukewarm to it, the thought of giving to the church, giving anything, is a once-a-year consideration, at year-end (for tax purposes) or at Easter, if at all.

If they do give, it is only out of a sense of obligation because it is the thing to do or there is an important tax deduction possible. Besides, argue those same persons, it is hard enough to make ends meet. My money has to go first for food and clothing and shelter for my family. If anything is left, and it seldom is, I will consider a gift to the church.

This is, of course, a natural concern. We all need to take care of our family responsibilities and to do so with the care that our love for them and theirs for us deserves. My wife and four children are important to me, and so I will and must care for them. Furthermore, I know that whatever I give to the church doesn't buy more food or toys or clothes nor put more money in the bank for me. Simple arithmetic tells me that.

As a Christian, I do have an obligation to buy all these things for my family, and I do. So goes the favorite argument against giving, especially giving off the top: "My income is simply not enough to buy what I need and still give it away. Let me pray and go to church and be a good Christian to my neighbor, but don't ask me to give. I simply cannot afford the luxury."

For most of us, at least those of us who are accustomed to giving generously, the question of giving is unnecessary. The question is not even raised. We give, and we give generously, because we believe in God and in the work of forgiveness and redemption of his Son for us. We believe God's word has been revealed to us in the Scriptures, and in those words we find his command to give. We believe in God. We take him at his word.

Read your New Testament: "Give, and it will be given

to you; good measure, pressed down, shaken together, running over, will be put into your lap. For the measure you give will be the measure you get back." (Luke 6:38)

Read Paul: "Each one must do as he has made up his mind, not reluctantly or under compulsion, for God loves a cheerful giver." (2 Cor. 9:7)

No question about it. Christians are literally commanded, or at least certainly expected, to give.

But why, other than that God has told us to? The law may be explicit, but the New Testament is Gospel, the Good News, the story of love. And love compels no one. So, we may give because of some anticipated or promised reward, if we must attach a reason to giving. After all, Malachi promised that God would "open the windows of heaven for you and pour down for you an overflowing blessing" whenever the "full tithes" were brought into his warehouse. (Malachi 3:10) Even Luke suggested "give, and it will be given to you." A reward determined by the measure of our generosity. Put him to the test, and God fulfills every need.

Or we take a long look around us and see the desperate needs of men and nations. And so we give to that. Our neighbor needs food and clothing. Our church needs a place to worship. We need a pastor to preach and teach. Our children need Christian training. Our church building is in dire need of repair. There is no end to the suffering and hunger and misery of the teeming millions all around the globe. No end of needs, desperate needs that cry out for our help.

And yet, that is not at all why I give or perhaps why you give either. Because whatever secondary reasons such as these may prompt me to give more and to give generously, the basic, underlying, transforming purpose for all that I give is the simple, yet powerful message of John 3:16: "For God so loved the world that he gave his only begotten Son, that whosoever believeth in him should not perish but have everlasting life."

Surely, if you believe in God and respect these words from John, there can be no more legitimate, authentic, primary motivation for your giving to God than this, that God loves you and gave his Son for you.

Which makes his gift of true love an expensive gift to me. With nothing less than grateful hearts Christians the world over, therefore, respond out of sheer gratitude for this gift, giving with whatever measure of love our human capacity is capable. If there were no promises of a reward, if there were not even any need for our gifts, indeed, even if the church closed its doors and worship ceased, the true believer could not help but still give. And he would do so generously simply because he is overwhelmingly grateful to God for his supreme gift of love. Inadequate as our response may sometimes seem to be, as paltry as our nickels and dimes and dollar bills may be, the Christian forever strives to do his best, always giving to God all that he has and is . . . and he does so all in loving response to that love from him.

Such then is the motivation to our giving. But then what are we actually going to give? How much must I give in dollars and cents and time and talents? Obviously, I cannot give what I do not have, but at the minimum I have at least myself to give. And surely that is a gift God will accept. Which means that all I am or have or hope to be, I give it and I do it for God. True, only a portion of my time and only some of my money will be specifically designated for God, but all the rest will be dedicated to him, used according to his will, devoted to his love for me. To give that way is evidence, I am convinced, of the highest order of Christian stewardship. Whatever we do, we do as unto God.

And so I work at my job as an honest, diligent Christian, intent on doing the best that I can. I deal with my neighbor in ways that reflect my Christian witness. I use my possessions, my money, my resources in ways that reflect a conviction born of living my life for Christ.

Yet the practical matter of how much of my silver and gold I give him is important, too. While everything I am or have is his and God expects me to take care of my own responsibilities and obligations, part of that money I earn is to be used to help others. If that love and gratitude prompt any response at all from me, I must decide as a practical matter how much I should really put into that offering plate on a Sunday morning and how much time I should spend on helping others (including my church) and how much of my ability and talent and skills I should give without expecting to be paid for it.

Again, read the New Testament: "On the first day of every week, each of you is to put something aside . . . as he may prosper (RSV), from what you have earned (The Living Bible), according to his financial ability (Phillips), as God has prospered him (KJV)."

In proportion, that is the key. The dollar amount I give in comparison to that given by the family in the pew next to me is not God's criteria. The proportion, the percentage of my income becomes the guide. Yet even then, some may not only give more dollars, but a greater percentage than I can . . . as God has prospered them.

This means that the family earning $200 a week may very well give twice as much, in dollars and cents, as the family earning only $100 a week. Likewise, the family that receives a pay raise or makes a handsome profit in a business deal or receives a bonus for inspiring sales techniques or safety procedures, will remember the Lord accordingly. And the family that suffers a loss or a catastrophe will continue giving proportionately, only the dollars and cents may be less.

Proportionate giving suggests a percentage of income without specifying the percentage or the dollar amount. And it sets no limits up or down. It is giving voluntarily without the threat of dues or a quota or a reward or merchandise in return. It is simply a measure of giving according to the decision each family makes on its own.

Of course, as noted previously, a Christian gives more than his money. He gives his time and his abilities, too. And it is important, I think, for a church to think beyond just the dollar signs when it goes out to inspire gifts for the annual budget. Because the family that gives unselfishly of itself is most likely the family that gives generously of its money as well. If you want more money for your church, you do not dare ask only for cash on the barrelhead. You must go out and ask for people, too.

As members give proportionately of their money, they can also give proportionately of their time, or at least ought to be encouraged to do so.

Each of us has a different amount of money but we all have twenty-four hours to the day. Theoretically we could, therefore, all give the same amount of time even though our dollar contribution might vary according to our prosperity. And we could give all our time, too, not just some small part of it. The Christian gives all his time, witnessing and serving whether he is on the job, or vacationing, or chatting with the neighbor across the back fence or baking pies for a church potluck.

But in so far as the organized church is the visible evidence of the Body of Christ on earth, how much time should we devote exclusively to activities in and for the church? Well, I find it difficult to think of a Christian as one who does not spend an hour or so in worship each week with fellow Christians. Another hour or so in a learning experience seems little enough to expect. If acts such as these are construed as giving time to the church, then at least that is a basic beginning.

But there is so much that needs to be done that can be done by the faithful. So, because we cherish the opportunity to worship in a church house, we paint and clean and care for it. Because we believe our children need training in the church, someone teaches. Ushers usher, choir members sing, tellers count the offering. And through it all the Word is preached by the pastor who reminds us that God is good, that God loves us, that God gave his Son and that we, his children, must give generously and gratefully in response to all of this. Out of the twenty-four hours available to each of us, surely our gratitude to God will require us to give some of that time specifically to him.

We give our money and we give our time. Likewise we give our talents. Believe me, there is really no end to the ways in which Christians can devote themselves to specific areas of the church's work. Whether to sing or teach, clean or sweep, visit or preach, follow or lead, it makes no matter; in whatever capacity we are able, we must give ourselves. And the Christian does.

Remember the parable of the talents? Jesus declares stern punishment for those who fail to apply their God-given talents to the work of the Kingdom, especially those whose talents are small and not outstanding. And to those who have received an abundance of talents, Jesus declares that very much will be required of them.

So, a Christian must give. He responds to God's love for him. And he gives in many ways. But this book is about money and this chapter is about giving more money. Specifically the emphasis here is on giving more money (thus more money for your church) by tithing, a method of proportionate giving.

But tithing set off all alone can be misinterpreted. The context within which it is discussed is all important. And so finally, halfway through this chapter, we finally talk about this important method of giving. It is important, I believe, to understand at the outset that tithing is not the be-all and end-all of giving. Set within the context of what it really means to give, a tithing emphasis can be an important part of the total stewardship program of a church and a very meaningful part of the Christian family's giving experience.

Before discussing a congregational program of emphasis on tithing (in order, at least in part, to get more money for your church), I think it may be useful to review the history of tithing, its Scriptural support, and its meaning for the active Christian family today.

According to the Rev. George W. Harrison in his book *Church Fund Raising* the history of tithing began long before the Bible came into being, cuts a path through it, notably in the Old Testament, and finally emerges in the teachings of the early church. References in the Bible are specific, but the path is not all that clear and precise. Even Jesus failed to make a clear and certain pronouncement about it.

Long before the authors of the Bible regarded the history of Israel as important, in fact about 3000 B.C., records show that the Egyptians paid tithes to their war gods. Many nations have paid tribute to such gods but the Egyptians specifically paid 10 percent of the spoils of war to their gods. That we know from their records.

No one seems to know exactly how the amount of 10 percent was chosen instead of 5 or 15 or 12½ percent. But 10 percent it was, perhaps because mathematically it is an easy percentage to figure. At any rate, according to Herodotus, the earliest Greek historian, it was Cyrus, the king of Persia in 559 B.C., who convinced his soldiers it would be a fine gesture of gratitude to offer one-tenth of the spoils of war to their supreme beings. It must have been an emotion-packed, inspiring plea, because the soldiers seem to have responded appropriately. Aside from the fact that their tithes were given in return for the gods' protection, the sinister truth of the matter is that Cyrus did not want any one of his soldiers getting richer than he. As a practical matter, someone had to accept all those trophies for the gods (obviously the gods weren't there to represent themselves), and Cyrus conveniently elected himself.

Throughout the annals of other nations—Babylon, Arabia, China, Greece—there is evidence that suggests their gods got their tithes, too. Tithing therefore has its roots back in the hazy dawn of history. It was not an invention of the Hebrews or the Christians.

According to Dr. Harrison, the first reported tithing in the Bible is by Abraham. Seems that on the way back home from his daring rescue of nephew Lot and his family, Abraham was challenged by that mysterious and puzzling priest, Melchizedek. Perhaps in a moment of weakness or maybe in the spirit of gratitude and generosity, he offered one-tenth of all that he had to the priest. It may have been the foreboding encounter that prompted Abraham to give one-tenth this time; at any rate, there is no record suggesting Abraham ever tithed again. In fairness to the record, however, tithing may have been such an accepted order of the day that the Biblical authors saw no need to report further on the personal finances of their leader.

The next reported tither is Jacob, grandson of Abraham. Teenagers those days had problem parents, too, and so Jacob ran away from home. His father disliked him and his brother was jealous of him. But Jacob found a good place to live in a strange land among strange people.

And there it was, in a dream one night, off in some lonely place, that he had a frightening experience. Yet, in spite of the fear of the dream, it must have pleased Jacob somehow because he interpreted it to mean that God would always be with him. So he made a promise to God: "Of all that thou shalt give me, I will surely give the tenth to thee." The outcome of that little episode was that Jacob became a tither and God prospered him.

From then on, the history of tithing becomes a bit hazy; a listing of the faithful who tithed never appears. Of course, tithing is mentioned prominently in the Mosaic regulations (Numbers 18:20–32). This was tithing by the Israelites to support the Levites, the spiritual servants of the people. In turn, the Levites tithed to support the high priest. Apparently the high priest kept all of his gifts for his own because the record fails to star his name as a tither on the annual membership list.

Then, according to Deuteronomy 14:22–27, during an annual nation-wide festival a tithe was exacted from the faithful. This time, though, it was a case of getting what you gave. Participants gave their tithe of livestock and then promptly took it back and ate it in the presence of the Lord.

On top of these kinds of tithing, there was also a third, this one required for the support of the needy—"the stranger, the fatherless, the widow."

And there were more. Consider the impact of Deuteronomy 12:6: "Thither you shall go, and thither you shall bring your burnt offerings and your sacrifices, your tithes and the offering that you present, your votive offerings, your freewill offerings and the firstlings of your herd and of your flock." Talk about a financial burden put upon the people by the ecclesiastical bureaucracy of that day! Three tithes (that is 30 percent) plus offerings and sacrifices to boot!

In the maze and confusion and hierarchical self-perpetuation of codes and rules and laws, the path of tithing history is lost in uncertainty. David and Solomon probably tithed. Amos admitted that the faithful tithed, but he called it a sham. Nehemiah urged tithers to rebuild the wall at Jerusalem, and Malachi pleaded for a return to God with tithes and faith.

Aside from these references to tithing, Old Testament support for it is sporadic and at best unclear. Yet, tithing was apparently an accepted practice of the day and an important expression by the faithful.

In the New Testament, the record is even less clear. Not

once does Jesus say, "Thou shalt tithe." In fact, he hardly refers to it at all except in passing. He may have talked a lot about money, but the parable of the Pharisee and the Publican (Luke 18:10–14) and Jesus' condemnation of the Pharisees' habits and attitudes (Matt. 23:23) are the only references He makes to tithing. And in both of these instances he only recites a current practice, neither encouraging nor discouraging it among his followers.

From the Church Fathers, though, there is support. Although tithing was still a voluntary act of giving in the third century when Cyprian taught, the attitude began to change. Tithing was the source of support for the poor and the clergy—with debate over who came first, clergy or poor. The preachings of Jerome and Ambrose and Augustine and Chrysostom, all in the fourth century, admonish, cajole and sometimes even threatèn the faithful to tithe. Eventually, at the Council of Tours, the tithe became official. In the ninth century it was civil law in the West.

With the rise and fall and struggles of papacies and western governments, the history of tithing in the Middle Ages continued to be confusing. But a hundred years or so ago it finally emerged once more as an important expression of commitment and dedication to the faith.

Thomas Kane, perhaps the most prominent layman in the tithing movement, recognized the importance of the tithe as an expression of faith and commitment. On his own he pushed the idea among fellow businessmen wherever he went. The Layman Tithing Foundation, an active, nonprofit organization, still carries on the teaching started by Kane. By now most major denominations in the United States have taken official action endorsing the concept of tithing as a significant expression of Christian faith.

Tithing is obviously a very important part of any fund raising emphasis. Yet many people object to the idea simply because too many congregations have legalized the concept. Too many parishioners have come to believe that tithing is a law of God and that if you fail to give God 10 percent you had better not expect God to give you his full blessing either. This kind of tithing is not tithing, or at least not the spirit of giving that Jesus encouraged.

If Malachi 3:10 and 2 Cor. 8:9 could be reconciled, that objection might be eliminated. Or rather, if the proponents of tithing would emphasize the latter instead of the former, reception of the tithing idea might be more palatable. Malachi 3:10 states: "Bring the full tithes into the storehouse, that there may be food in my house; and thereby put me to the test, says the Lord of hosts, if I will not open the windows of heaven for you and pour down for you an overflowing blessing." 2 Cor. 8:9 recalls: "For you know the grace of our Lord Jesus Christ, that though he was rich, yet for your sake he became poor, so that by his poverty you might become rich."

It is a spontaneous response to this overflowing love of Jesus Christ for us that prompts the Christian to give, and to give 10 percent or more. The Christian does not respond to the law when he gives; he responds to the love and joy that are part of the act of giving. If he gives 10 percent, very good. But when he gives proportionately and when he does so with love and joy, then he has fulfilled all that Christ asks, no matter how many or how few dollars happen to represent that percentage.

When I am told that I *must* tithe, my gift is no longer an offering, it is a tax. When I am told that the only measure of my gift to the church will be my tithe, I object. Jesus commended the widow for her mite. Zaccheus paid back all those whom he had wronged. Were these tithes? If not, did Jesus reject them?

Jesus had nothing to say about the size of those gifts

or any others. It was the spirit that counted, the attitude, the motivation that made the gift acceptable.

It is obvious that the financial impact on the church could be tremendous if everyone tithed. It doesn't take a computer to be able to figure out what that would mean to the crimped budgets of many a beleaguered church treasury. But not everyone has caught the vision of what substantial, generous giving can do for their lives. Until they do, I will object to forcing them to give more than they are ready to give. The church has a responsibility to teach and explain and inspire and motivate, but it cannot compel.

Tithing is not a bargain we strike with God—"I will give 10 percent just to make sure I can keep the other 90 percent." God has not signed any promissory note offering a return for my tithe. I object to the notion that just because I tithe, therefore, my business is bound to get better. It may, at least my attitude will improve with tithing, but my business may go as flat as a doornail.

To use tithing as a gimmick for giving is equally a mistake. To promote nine weeks of tithing misses the point. To promote year-long tithing hits at the center. If our emphasis is motivated just to get more people to give more dollars in order to ease the bind on the church's bank account, I object. It is just another trick to get more money for the church.

No matter how desperately the church may need more money, I object to using tithing as the springboard to meet a budget deficit. Tithing must be voluntary. It must be a personal decision. It must be a matter of deep prayer and study, a way to give to God without pressure from others. Tithing is a way of bringing spiritual joy to the giver. And that, it seems to me, is a prime requisite for any religious experience. For those who do not tithe, that joy will be difficult to comprehend.

I am convinced that proportionate giving is one of the most effective and favorable ways of financing the church programs. When proportionate giving reaches the tithing percentage and then goes beyond it, there will be more money for your church. And it will be given joyfully and generously.

To tithe or not to tithe may be a good question, but the real issue is a personal one, whether to give or not to give . . . and then how much to give. Tithing and beyond may be the answer, eventually. But no matter how small or insignificant our money or our talents may seem to us (Jesus did recognize the widow's mite and the little man's talent), we can and must use them in the time that God has given us for his purposes and his kingdom. And we do so, not because God expects or requires us to do so, but because he loves us and we are extremely grateful to him.

A PROGRAM OF TITHING EMPHASIS

In every congregation there are several levels of commitment to tithing already evident:

1. There are those who may already be tithers. Your efforts at a congregational program will help to reinforce their existing conviction.

2. There are those who have never tithed, but who are sincere and generous givers anyway. They are willing to grow in their giving. Your congregational program will help them the most in accepting tithing as a standard toward which they will begin to work.

3. And there are those others who will literally dig in and absolutely resist any mention of tithing because their minds are already made up and closed. Somewhere in the past they have picked up a wrong notion of what tithing is all about. They have been "turned off" by it all. Perhaps

your program will help to show them the right way. At least you can try; just don't expect miracles right away.

You will want to concentrate your efforts on the first two groups. They will be the most receptive. And then, perhaps, some of what you say and what they do will rub off on the third group, the hard shells. If so, it will certainly be for the good of their stewardship attitudes.

Leadership commitment—It is essential, if you expect to present this program on tithing convincingly to your congregation, that the minister and the official board be in agreement on the subject. Not all of them have to be tithers, although that would certainly help, of course. But it is not likely to be the case. Don't wait for the miracle to happen. Just make sure that the minister and the official board are committed to the position that tithing is a valid standard toward which they will work, and that they are willing to say this to the congregation.

Official board action—You will need almost a full meeting of the official board to get your program ideas accepted by that group. You cannot hurry through simply to get official action, because tithing is a subject that can be dealt with best on a person-to-person basis, where individuals can respond to each other and the group.

Ask the chairman to block out at least one hour for your presentation at the beginning of a meeting. Then go after getting a commitment to be involved.

Don't lecture for that hour; but get the participants talking, responding to thoughts and ideas that you introduce. Don't push yourself off as an expert or an authority on tithing. You are simply one member of a congregation talking with other members about an important principle of giving. You may want to witness of your tithing, but you and the group all have the same objective here—to help individuals in your congregation to grow spiritually. A person's attitude toward giving is part and parcel of spiritual growth.

Your own agenda should go something like this: state the subject, then use a question to get discussion started. Give your own tithing definition. Offer some Biblical background. Stimulate more discussion on tithing today. Finally, seek a commitment to tithing as a principle.

The previous discussions in this chapter (and book) will offer considerable resource materials for your discussion. Some of the materials listed in the Bibliography at the end of the book will offer additional help. Check through this listing of Scriptural references: Leviticus 27:30, Psalm 24:1, Proverbs 3:9, Malachi 3:10, Luke 12:34, Acts 20:35, Ephesians 2:10.

Get the participants to express their own attitudes and ideas about tithing. Correct any that seem negative or misleading or inaccurate. Personal witness from tithers can be extremely useful at this point.

Remind the group that the commitment to go along with such a program does not mean additional committees or staff appointments. You already have an Every Member Response program going. A tithing emphasis fits neatly into the educational part of that plan. Use that program to encourage greater giving and more enthusiastic participation through tithing.

A tithing program is not something you do apart from the rest of the life of the congregation. It is simply the way you go about encouraging members to think of their giving as you stimulate consideration of their pledge for the coming year.

Group Meetings—At some point in your program, once you've gotten started, you may want to encourage the gathering of small groups to talk about tithing as a standard for giving. Approach the discussion much the same as you did for the official board. Ask questions, stimulate discussion and get commitments that aim for tithing.

Home visits, individual presentations and printed materials can all be useful. Promotional materials must be ordered from denominational headquarters sufficiently in advance to have them on hand several weeks for study and planning.

Commitment Sunday—Your aim is to concentrate on commitment Sunday, that day when you and the members of your congregation make a commitment on giving for the coming year. Plan your strategy in advance, and then as commitment Sunday draws closer, develop an ongoing enthusiasm that will culminate in more members than ever before making their tithe commitment.

Remember that a tithing emphasis is not just another program. And it is not just for one year. It is an emphasis that will be continuing for a long time, or at least should be. It has been around a long time, and I suspect it is here to stay. Some of your members will exceed the tithe, others will only get a bit closer this year, but eventually they, too, will reach out to the full tithe you have been encouraging all along. And some people won't ever get there.

Nevertheless, it is good stewardship to hold up tithing as a standard of giving before your people all the time. The fruits of a spiritual awakening in the new tither are worth waiting for.

CHAPTER FOUR

How to Find More Money For Your Church

There are probably as many different programs available for raising money for the church as there are congregations trying to raise more money. While many plans are similar, congregations are different and so their fund raising techniques will be different, too. Needs, people, experiences—these all vary and each may require some kind of unique approach to getting more money for the church. No readymade program is likely to fit one situation to a T. Thus the detailed outlines in this chapter are not likely to be used step-by-step, or item-by-item, by any congregation.

But the outlines represent a plan, and a plan is crucial to the success of any effort. Even no plan is a plan, although its outcome might be predictably disastrous. If you do not want disaster and if you want a generous response from your membership, a plan of action is necessary.

Now, as I have pointed out, plans vary tremendously. They range from the simplest of "grace giving" plans (no pledges and little or no formal program of any kind) to the most elaborate plans carried out by professional fund-raising firms. Either of these plans, or one of those inbetween, may be exactly the plan needed in some congregation, perhaps even your own. It all depends upon the nature of your congregation, its leadership and the motivation that inspires your people to give.

This chapter, indeed this whole book, assumes that most congregations need to use a rather elaborate plan for raising money. Here, then, are probably more ideas than you can use, but you can pick and choose according to your own needs.

Now, a fund raising program must be more than just an attempt to get more money for your church. All kinds of groups and organizations raise money and they do it many ways, often with a certain amount of high pressure arm-twisting as they cite desperate needs, dire consequences, civic obligations and personal responsibilities as justification for more than token giving. Surely the church has its own long list of needs, but giving for the sake of meeting needs in the church is not, to my way of thinking anyway, a legitimate goal, as Chapter 3 clearly points out. A Christian is motivated to give because he needs to give. That comes first. Then, when he gives, that giving meets the needs of the church, whether to pay pastors and benevolences, or provide for Christian training and paving of parking lots.

Unless an attitude of responsible stewardship permeates the giving attitudes of the members of your church, you may as well copy the fund raising program of the local YMCA or United Way or Heart Fund. Stewardship, Christian stewardship, is at the heart of Christian giving. And it must be at the heart of the fund raising program in your church, too, if your program is going to lift sights as well as dollars.

Stewardship obviously means different things to different people. To some it says money, pure and simple. To others it means tithing or at least proportionate giving. To some it is a bad word, to others only distasteful; for many, it is a very good and important word. Important, because to many of us, stewardship is a full life process. Thus "the stewardship of life" says to me that Christian stewardship is the response I make to everything in life. It is more than money. It is all of life. And that, I think, is important to say and understand.

The stewardship response I may make personally with my life and abilities and resources is not the same as the stewardship response my congregation may make. Personal and corporate stewardship should be distinguished. My personal stewardship is represented in the attitudes and intentions of what I have and own. The stewardship responsibility of my congregation must fulfill the purposes for which the church exists as expressed by the intentions of its many donors and supporters.

A congregation's stewardship attitudes, unlike my own, will be reflected in the manner in which it pays its benevolences, its pastors, and its other obligations. It is reflected in the percentages of total dollars available spent for Christian education or cleaning supplies or debt retirement. It can even be measured by how well and how often the church's physical plant is used, by what is spent on postage, or by how the pastor's time and energy are used. Can he visit and preach and counsel, or is he forever turning the mimeograph crank, sweeping floors and folding bulletins? The measure of a congregation's stewardship attitudes can be determined by the way it spends its dollars and uses its resources of people and plans. And that attitude is there for all to see. An individual's stewardship is measured by the way he gives himself—all that he is or hopes to be—and it may not all be seen by men.

Thus an individual's attitude toward the stewardship of his life must permeate his giving. And all the fund raising programs in the world will not be successful unless Christians are educated to their responsibility to give, which, as we will see, is the second step in a successful fund raising effort.

One of the best ways in which people can be motivated toward an appropriate stewardship attitude is by reminding them of their basic Christian conviction—I believe in God the Father, God the Son, and God the Holy Spirit. That is the Apostles' Creed, of course. And as with any creed, it has consequences for those who say it, or at least it ought to have consequences. For when I profess my Christian faith in the words of that historic creed, I am also setting forth certain basic convictions about the stewardship of my life.

I am saying, in so many words, that as a child of God, I must react to what God has done for me through his creation, redemption, and sanctification of my life. That response is my stewardship of life.

A STEWARDSHIP OF LIFE

Simply put, I believe that God has created the world, and that because he created it I believe that he is the owner of everything that exists, and that he has made me a caretaker, a manager, a steward over that small portion of creation he has given to me to use.

I for one must admit that I do not always act as if that is what I believe. My own self-centeredness, my own forgetfulness, indeed my own selfishness, make me forget and I begin to think that the whole world around me is mine to control as I wish, if I can; to manage God's creatures as though they were my own, if I can manage them; and to treat all the things God has created as though they were mine, if I can make enough money to possess them.

Yet, in my better, God-directed moments, I realize that the house I may have bought is not mine but God's; that the car I drive may be registered in my name, but it is actually his; that even the clothes on my back were provided by him; that the money in the bank is there by the sweat and toil of my effort, to be sure, but that God has blessed me with the abilities to earn it; that even my own children are a blessing and a heritage from God. In fact, when you get right down to it, you soon realize, or at least I do, that all I am or have or ever hope to be I owe basically not to myself, my parents, my teachers, my associates, or even to my circumstances, but to my loving heavenly Father.

And because I believe this, I must act as a steward. If I continue to use the earth and those things God has given me, I must do so with the care it deserves because it is not mine. In a very real sense, it has simply been loaned to me to use for a little while. I farm corn or raise cattle, I handle stocks and bonds or keep books, I sweep the floor or wait tables or sell groceries, I push a pencil or work a machine—all in the certainty that I am using not my own but the Lord's equipment. My paycheck and bankbook are more than paper and figures. They tell how much of all his silver and gold the Lord has put at my disposal. And so I return a reasonable proportion of it directly to him by giving to his church. As a New Testament caretaker I want to give not only the first and the best, but also the most, 10 percent or more, as God may have prospered me. And only then do I invest the rest in everything from groceries to gasoline, from clothes to cars, from books to bonds, all as an agent, handling that which really is not mine after all, but for which I am very much responsible.

When I read about the resurrection of my Lord on that

first Easter Day, I, too, am apt to say with Thomas: "My Lord and my God!" And then believe along with the rest of the disciples that "because he lives, I, too, shall live!"

Of course, I would be the first to admit that I do not always live like a person who has been redeemed and saved. More often than not I use my body as if it were my own, and not God's, to do with as I pleased. I don't always ask him where he wants me to go, or what he wants me to do or how I ought to think and act. To be completely honest, there are times when I don't even think about God.

But the Bible is quite specific in telling me that I am not my own, however much I may want to believe otherwise. Instead, it tells me that I was redeemed and that I am to glorify God with my body. I am to live as Christ's steward with the body, mind and soul he has redeemed. My body is his and I am to use it to praise him, to speak for him, to witness to his saving and keeping grace. That is the life I owe.

When I stop ignoring God and resisting him, I learn that in mercy he has called me through the Gospel and his Word, and caused sin and grace to make sense to me. What is more, he continues to call me, he keeps on enlightening me, he constantly causes me to grow in grace and in the knowledge of my Lord and Saviour Jesus Christ, and he keeps me from falling so that he will be able to present me without blemish before the presence of his glory with rejoicing. And all this he does for me although I don't deserve any of it.

Furthermore, whatever work God has in store for me he does right here, right here in this temple of the Holy Spirit, here in my body. Wherever I go there is the Holy Spirit. When I need courage, the Holy Spirit gives it to me. When I am faced with temptation, the Holy Spirit gives me the power to withstand. When I need hope, the Holy Spirit assures me of the God of all hope. When I need peace, the Holy

Spirit gives it. In the midst of every trial and temptation, suffering and disappointment, heartache and heartbreak, there is the Holy Spirit with me. He is with me in every moment, in every up or down of life.

Furthermore, if I believe that God works in me like that, I will not be able to keep him all to myself. I will be compelled to tell other people about what he is doing to me. I have a stewardship here that I cannot avoid, for the Holy Spirit kept bottled up inside of me will soon be smothered and dead if I do not venture out to share God's love for me with my neighbor.

And so you see, I cannot worship God with a Sunday offering that is a mere token of my appreciation. Instead, I must give him all that I can, for I honestly believe that God has created me and given me the resources I have, and that I am responsible to him for everything I have. And because God has redeemed me, whatever response I make is small response indeed to his gift for me on a cross. Even then what I may think is too much for me to give is never enough, really, for him. Furthermore, I believe I would be committing a sin if my gift were not a generous one of love and devotion and amount according to my ability, because only as the Holy Spirit calls me into this great fellowship, this Christian Church, this Communion of Saints, am I redeemed and made perfect for my father in heaven.

God the Father, Son and Holy Spirit, the Godhead in One, the blessed Trinity, has given me a far more abundant stewardship than the tiny offering I may give to him on a Sunday morning for the work of his church. For that kind of stewardship goes far beyond my pocketbook. It involves my very being, my life, my all. And this much I give him, all that I am, little enough as it is for his kingdom, because this is what I believe!

At least that is the way I see it.

A STEWARDSHIP DESCRIPTION

Dr. Raymond Olson has written in his book *Stewards Appointed* that "Christian stewardship is the response of the Christian to God's love and purpose, the recognition that he is appointed by God to use his life responsibly, productively and thankfully. This is his stewardship because Christ died for him. It is possible because Christ has risen.

"God clearly intends that the Christian shall develop and use his capacities, his abilities and his precious years. Placed in a material world, he is to share in managing and using it so as to serve God and the human family for which it was created.

"All the best fruits of the centuries have been entrusted to the Christian, as a member of this family, including worthy institutions of religion, government, education and scientific research. He is called to use this material, moral and spiritual inheritance for the enrichment of his own generation and generations not yet born.

"Above all, the Christian is a steward of the Gospel—the sacred revelation of the will of God for man through Jesus Christ. He is called to devote regularly generous portions of his time, money, and all other available resources for the present and future proclamation of this Gospel, and to join eagerly with others in carrying out this supreme mission."

Stewardship consists of God's act of sovereign love and man's response in faith and love, personally, in his own giving, and, collectively, through the giving of his church.

The Scriptures abound with reference to that love and man's responsible response. Try these:

Genesis 1:26	Ephesians 2:19
Genesis 1:28	I Cor. 14:12
Isaiah 53:6	I Peter 4:10

Romans 6:23	Hebrews 10:24
John 3:16	Ephesians 2:10
John 1:12,13	John 14:12
II Cor. 5:21	II Cor. 8 and 9
Ephesians 1:5	I Cor. 16:2
John 17:16–18	Matthew 10:8b
John 20:21b	Luke 12:48b
Matthew 28:19	Romans 14:12
Romans 10:14–15a	Romans 11:29

Develop those attitudes yourself, recognize the importance of motivating your membership in the same way, and you will have taken a basic step toward generating a successful fund-raising campaign.

Taking for granted that stewardship, as described thus far, is a vital and necessary concern of the church and that its practice in the lives of Christians and their congregations is a good and acceptable thing, we proceed to the plan—the nuts and bolts of getting more money for your church through fund raising.

A PLAN

First off you have to get organized. That is, you must develop an organizational plan of people and assign specific responsibilities. Otherwise, everyone will be running off in ten different directions doing ten different things. Coordination comes through proper organization. And the place to begin is with an overall central committee headed up by a dynamic, energetic competent person.

It's the responsibility of this stewardship committee to raise the money. A finance committee is responsible for planning the budget and spending the money, or at least seeing that it is spent properly. But the stewardship committee develops the ongoing, year-round stewardship program of the church as well as the annual intensive affair, too. Its membership will include the pastor and key lay leaders. A working core of six to nine should be sufficient. Subcommittees will include a lot of other people eventually. The membership of the committee is important. Pick the right persons at the very beginning.

And so what does a stewardship committee really do?

WHAT DOES A STEWARDSHIP COMMITTEE DO?

Effective, enthusiastic, successful stewardship programs do not just happen. They are planned. One of the best ways to get that planning done is with a year-round, action-minded stewardship committee of the most effective leadership talent you can muster, meeting every month, planning all year.

The capstone, of course, of any stewardship program is the annual canvass, or every member response or visit. By itself, that is not the stewardship program, but it is certainly the climax of all the planning and promotion and praying done during the rest of the year. The success of the program, indicated by the annual canvass, is dependent on church members' attitudes as they are developed and cultivated by your committee all year long.

An effective committee must have objectives toward which it works and by which its progress can be measured. It must fulfill its responsibilities. Reading the list of responsibilities in the following paragraph is a way for the committee to start. You will want to expand or clarify this list according to your own needs.

What are the responsibilities of your stewardship committee? They ought to be to promote, encourage, lead and develop in all your church members a higher level of proportionate giving for the Lord's work. That is basic, and perhaps obvious. To accomplish that objective, the committee is responsible for promoting expressions of Christian faith in daily living, for teaching the Christian use of money, for interpreting the congregation's local, church-wide and worldwide work and—perhaps most visibly—for conducting the annual canvass or visitation.

To test the effectiveness of that program, the committee's work can be regularly evaluated by 1) the increase in the level of giving by members to the total budget and program of the congregation, and 2) the increase in the level of giving by members to benevolence and other programs beyond the work of their own parish.

The stewardship committee must do more than just meet in October to plan an annual visit or solicitation of commitments. That alone is important and a very necessary step, but the potential for raising the giving sights of members depends on more than that. Here is how your committee may want to begin work on the yearlong meetings and planning.

First of all, schedule regular monthly meetings of the committee. And be specific about time, place, dates and purposes. A reminder notice ten days ahead of a meeting helps. Distribute agendas and make appointments for a recorder, devotional leaders and Bible study persons well in advance of each meeting. Then plan the meeting carefully.

—Start on time; end on time.

—Study in depth one aspect of the stewardship program. Review principles, methods, and procedures.

—Review and evaluate the stewardship program to date. How are things going? Are objectives being met? Are pledges being paid? Is planning on schedule for the Fall's visitation program?

—Review plans for publicizing the current status of giving by church members.

—Plan ahead. Set congregational stewardship goals a year in advance. Make specific plans for the next four months. Consider objectives, programs, personnel, promotional materials, timing and publicity.

—Assign specific responsibilities to committee members and follow up with their reports at the next meeting.

—Announce the next meeting date. Adjourn. Promptly distribute minutes of the meeting. Report to your official board.

But what should you do at those meetings? Well, for example, in April you should already be planning the direction of your Fall program. Do you have a chairman? Does your committee have its objectives clearly in mind? Is your time schedule set and cleared with your official board? Is machinery in motion to get personnel, publicity, dates and places all set up, ready to go?

In May you might make plans to visit new members received during the Spring. It is time for a special letter to the congregation reporting giving trends thus far this year and urging continued support during the summer months. A final report on plans for the Fall program should be the top monthly meeting agenda item.

In June you will need to follow up on plans for the Fall program, review giving records to date, attend stewardship and finance committee workshops. Then, during July and August, planning for your Fall program moves into high gear. It is too late to make plans in October. Between April and the end of the summer is the time. Make the most of these summer months to gather information and plan and prepare.

In September your committee needs to keep on building up to the annual visit. You can work with your Christian education staff on ways to stimulate and interpret stewardship attitudes among the children. As the new school year begins, develop plans for getting your stewardship message into your Sunday church-school program.

The October committee meeting is crucial. Check the momentum of the proposed visitation program. Are you building up enthusiasm and interest for a successful every-home visit or congregational dinner or special worship service or cottage meetings? Is publicity on schedule? Are visitors trained? Is your promotion thorough, intensive and professionally done? Are there loose ends?

Finally, in November, the planning that began in April culminates in your annual program emphasis. Keep up the momentum until your response is complete. Then report enthusiastically to the members. Tell them how they did.

Report the final results of your program in December to your official board. Help plan next year's budget and its promotion. In January, you will get the final, completed results of your Fall program efforts. Report to the annual congregational meeting. Begin plans now and order materials for any Spring follow-up visits or other stewardship promotion. If necessary, reorganize the stewardship committee with members recently elected or appointed.

In February and March, your committee should review unresponsive member lists, visit new members, report on giving trends and keep the official board informed of progress. At every turn, committee members should be talking stewardship wherever they can—in meetings, with new member classes, in "temple talks" at the church services, in the parish newsletter, etc.

No program will be the same in any two congregations. You will obviously have to adapt your own format, using whatever appropriate parts of the many excellent programs are available to you. For specific suggestions for your Fall program, you can contact your own denominational headquarters. But no matter what your program, its success depends on an active committee doing things all year, even this month, too.

Plan ahead, publicize, promote, pray. Effective stewardship programs do not just happen. They are planned. And an active committee is the key to success.

THE DETAILS FOR YOUR PROGRAM

So much for the overall picture. You now have an idea of what your stewardship committee is supposed to do all year as it builds up its plans and momentum for the Fall giving program. (If your church year begins some other month rather than January, you will need to shift your planning accordingly.)

Actually, as is evident from what your stewardship committee is supposed to do, the Every Member Response (as I prefer to call it rather than a canvass or fund raising activity or even visitation) is not just a once-a-year activity. It is really a yearlong program of preparation, implementation and follow-up. While the intensive part of that program is jammed into a busy six weeks, normally from about the first of October to the middle of November (or from the first of May to the middle of June for June 30 fiscal year congregations), planning for the program goes on in Spring and Summer, too, with constant evaluation, study and planning, all aimed toward that late Fall crisis time.

The basic plan, as I see it, can be divided into five distinct steps—preparation, programming, education, response and evaluation. And it can work something like this.

While the immediate objective of the Every Member Response (EMR) is to get financial commitments (responses) from the membership in order to underwrite the programs of the congregation for the next year, the real objective is to educate the members about the programs of the church and to get as many as possible actively involved in those programs. Regardless of the financial results, if you have gotten people involved and motivated their attitudes about stewardship, and if they have learned more about the life and work of their church, you have made progress.

It is a mistake to count success only in terms of the dollars and cents raised. That may be what you want. It is certainly what you need. But don't overlook those important by-products of a deeper commitment, greater involvement and better understanding achieved by those who respond. An intensive EMR is bound to involve many people and create some important and lasting gains in more than just dollars.

Step 1. Preparation.

What kind of program will the church have? What will be the time schedule? What activities will be included? Will visits be made or a congregational dinner held or pledges simply placed on the altar? Who will take charge of each event? What committees are required? When do we begin and what dates should be involved in this specific emphasis? Planning begins six months before visits are made. Eventually, a week by week calendar of events, activities, mailings, brochures and visits must be worked out.

To initiate the planning, the pastor and the stewardship committee will huddle together to select various EMR committee chairmen and other personnel. Promotional materials will be ordered.

Planning also includes the gathering of facts, trends and statistical data that will be useful in developing the program and making the visits schedule. It is information that will tell the story of what has gone on before, where the congregation has been, and how it has responded in the past. While such statistics will note trends, they are not intended to forecast future performance. As you can tell from the illustrative material that follows, the statistical data is extensive, but it is important for planning.

And so the details are laid out, the facts are gathered, leaders are chosen, and the plan begins to unfold. The campaign is underway.

FACTS AND TRENDS YOU WILL NEED TO KNOW FOR YOUR STEWARDSHIP EMPHASIS

1. Our congregation has _____ has not _____ conducted an Every Member Response for its current operating budget.

2. If "Yes," state when last visiting was done _____

3. How many persons comprised the EMR General Committee? _____

4. How many workers were enlisted? _____

5. If another method of securing pledges was used, what was it?

6. How many members of the congregation pledged the last time? _____

7. How many did not make a pledge? _____

8. Membership	Preceding 3, 5, or 10 years	Last full year	Increase
All baptized members			
Adults only			

9. Considering all the individuals in our congregation, the members would fall percentage-wise into the following age brackets: Young (to 35) ____% Middle-aged (36–59) ____% Elderly (60+) ____%

10. By occupation we are: (list principal occupations):

_____

11. What percentage of the congregation pledged? #6, divided by #6 + #7 _____%

12. Weekly Giving Pattern by Families

Actual Weekly Gift	Number of Gifts	Percentage of Gifts	Weekly Total	Yearly Total
$75+				
$50+				
$35+				
$25+				
$20+				
$15+				
$12.50+				
$10+				
$7.50+				
$5+				
$4+				
$3.50+				
$2.50+				
$2+				
$1+				
Less				
No gift of record				
TOTAL	______	______	______	______

13. What is the percent of "No gift of record"? _____%

14. Our Budget:

	Last Year	Current Year	Percent Attained Last year
For current expenses	$	$	%
For special local purposes			
For benevolences and others			
Total of loose plate			
Total other offerings			
TOTALS	$	$	%

15. Our Expenditures:

	Last Year	Current Year (to date)	Percent Anticipated This year
For current expenses	$	$	%
For special local expenses			
For benevolences and others			
TOTALS	$	$	%

16. Is there now a cash deficit? ________ If so, how much? ________

17. Is a deficit anticipated by the end of the year? ______ If so, how much, and what contributed to the condition? ______

18. Our pledges:

	Amount Pledged	Budget	Percent of Budget Pledged
For current expenses	$	$	%
For special local purposes			
For benevolences and others			
TOTAL PLEDGED	$	$	%

19. Number family units to reach in Every Member Response this year: ______

20. Number of envelope sets in use this year: ______

21. Indebtedness: $______ for ______

22. Our Resources:

	Family Units		Family Income Units
Husband and wife both members, at least one full income (include all children not working)	______	@ 1	______
Fully employed unmarried members	______	@ 1	______
Wife only member	______	@ ½	______
Mixed marriage (two denominations)	______	@ ⅓	______
Restricted income—retirement, etc.	______	@ ¼	______
TOTALS	______		______(A)

23. The average income per family of our congregation is estimated at $______. The average income for our city ______ is estimated at $______ (annually).

24. Total family income units (A) above ______ multiplied by average family income $______ equals total resources $______ (B).

15% of $______(B) = $______
10% of $______ = $______
6% of $______ = $______
5% of $______ = $______
4% of $______ = $______
3% of $______ = $______
2½% of $______ = $______
2% of $______ = $______

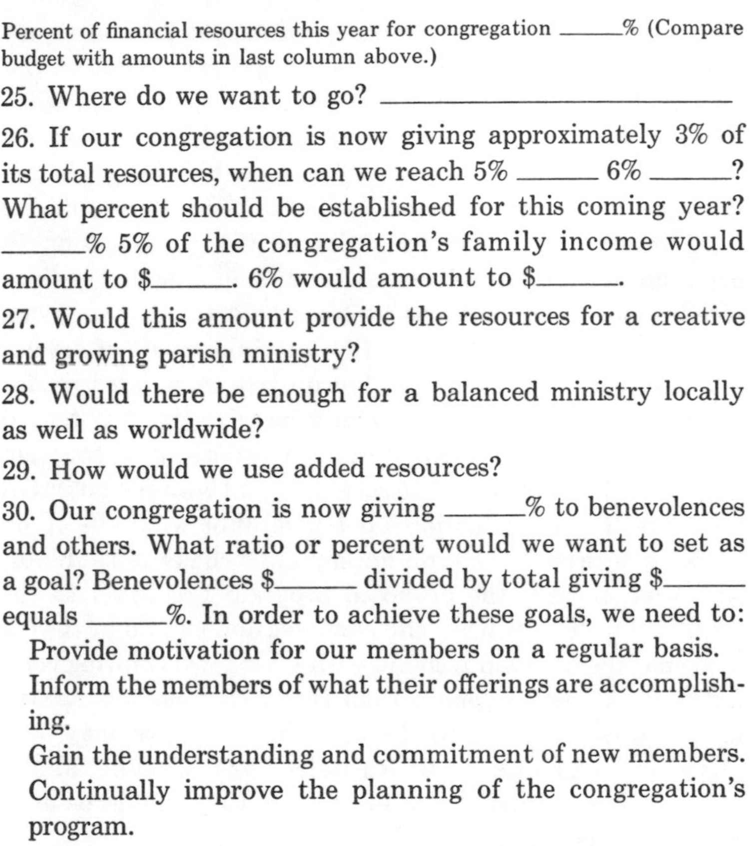

Percent of financial resources this year for congregation ______% (Compare budget with amounts in last column above.)

25. Where do we want to go? ______________________________

26. If our congregation is now giving approximately 3% of its total resources, when can we reach 5% ______ 6% ______? What percent should be established for this coming year? ______% 5% of the congregation's family income would amount to $______. 6% would amount to $______.

27. Would this amount provide the resources for a creative and growing parish ministry?

28. Would there be enough for a balanced ministry locally as well as worldwide?

29. How would we use added resources?

30. Our congregation is now giving ______% to benevolences and others. What ratio or percent would we want to set as a goal? Benevolences $______ divided by total giving $______ equals ______%. In order to achieve these goals, we need to:

Provide motivation for our members on a regular basis.

Inform the members of what their offerings are accomplishing.

Gain the understanding and commitment of new members.

Continually improve the planning of the congregation's program.

Step 2. Programming.

With the completion of the preceding study, the second step of the program swings into high gear. The program committee meets to lay out what all the congregation ought to be doing next year and how much it may cost. Some time during the first two weeks of the active program, nearly 10 percent of the membership (a good cross section) will be called together for three important sessions. They will analyze and scrutinize the current program of the church from finances to nursery care, from replacing the roof to repairing the furnace, from changing the choir's location to remodeling the basement for a teen room. In other words, the program committee will ask 10 percent of the members: What is the congregation doing with the resources it now has and what should it be doing to fulfill its mission as church members?

In session one the committee evaluates the goals and programs of the congregation. In session two the committee examines the leadership potential of the congregation to determine what is possible with what is available. In the third meeting, the group will first attempt to estimate the giving potential of the congregation (by any one or all of several different methods). Then it will formulate some priorities for a program proposal. Once it determines the giving potential of the congregation, it estimates, from among all its program proposals, those that could be accomplished with the potential resources. The congregation's potential, not what the trend of giving suggests, but the potential, is matched against needs. And that, then, is the proposed program presented to the membership. This is what the congregation can do next year if the membership will respond with loving, overflowing commitment. A lesser response than this goal means reduction in the proposed program. Final giving response may well exceed last year's total, but if it falls short of potential and of the program proposal, not everything that should be done is going to get done.

Having matched potential resources and program priorities, the committee disbands and step two is completed.

CHECK LIST FOR THE PLANNING COMMITTEE

	O.K.	Needs Attention	No Need	Don't Know
Christian Education				
1. Sunday church school program meets needs of				

	O.K.	Needs Attention	No Need	Don't Know
congregation and community?				
2. Vacation church-school program?				
3. Released time program (if available)?				
4. Training program for prospective teachers?				
5. Fulltime personnel needed?				
6. Audio-visuals under responsible direction?				
7. Subsidies for training, schools and retreats?				
8. Library facilities for membership?				
9. Adult counselors for youth activities?				
10. Promote church colleges and church vocations?				
11. Promote reading of official denomination publication?				
Evangelism				
1. Instruction and orientation for new members?				
2. Assimilate new members into congregational life?				
3. Use local news and broadcast media?				

	O.K.	Needs Attention	No Need	Don't Know
4. Outreach to church-school parents?				
5. Reach new people in community promptly?				
6. Effective use made of materials provided by the church?				
7. Contacts maintained with our youth in colleges and armed services?				
8. Periodic congregational fellowship gatherings?				
9. Leadership trained in evangelism?				
10. Members prepared for witnessing in daily life?				
Ministry				
1. Staff sufficient for present and expected opportunities?				
2. Pastor relieved of administrative detail?				
3. Organized voluntary service program?				
4. Good working facilities for entire staff?				
5. Salaries of entire staff reviewed annually?				

	O.K.	Needs Attention	No Need	Don't Know
6. Congregation regularly informed through parish newsletter?				
7. Periodic evaluation of program and outreach of congregation?				
Property				
1. Housekeeping (e.g., cleanliness, heating, etc.)?				
2. Bulletin boards and signs?				
3. Custodial?				
4. Repairs made promptly?				
Worship				
1. Present hours of services adequate?				
2. Attendance by family units stressed?				
3. Hymnals in adequate supply and repair?				
4. Music leadership and staff?				
5. Organ and instruments on regular maintenance?				
6. Choir supplies and facilities?				
7. Ushers friendly, helpful and attentive?				

	O.K.	Needs Attention	No Need	Don't Know
8. Members cordial to one another and to visitors?				
9. Religious art, music, and drama appreciation cultivated?				
10. Frequency of the Sacraments?				
Social Ministry				
1. Congregational program of Christian service?				
2. Service to emotionally disturbed (in the community)?				
3. Service to physically handicapped (blind, deaf, etc.)?				
4. Laity trained to visit and aid the sick, shut-ins and aged?				
5. Special transportation assistance?				
6. Laity serving as volunteers in local institutions?				
7. Interpret social problems?				
8. Hospitality to international students?				
Stewardship				
1. Stewardship education a year-round concern?				

	O.K.	Needs Attention	No Need	Don't Know
2. Stewardship is understood to be total life commitment?				
3. Effective use is made of time and abilities of members?				
4. Children's pledges encouraged and offering envelopes used?				
5. Proportionate giving stressed?				
6. Our congregation is moving toward increased benevolence support?				
7. Mission education programs sponsored?				
8. Visits made to new members for information and pledges?				
Finance				
1. Prepares inclusive budget in view of expressed objectives for the congregation?				
2. Gives oversight to all financial affairs of the congregation?				
3. Attends, through the treasurer, to the prompt payment of all obligations?				
4. Benevolence monies are forwarded each month to the proper agencies?				
5. "Overage" giving considered?				

A TYPICAL PARISH PROGRAM PROPOSAL

			Percentage of total
Parish Extension			
1. Benevolences	$20,000		
2. Other benevolences	1,000		
		$21,000	27.5
Parish Expansion			
1. Christian education	$ 2,000		
2. Evangelism and social ministry	1,000		
3. Youth activities	700		
4. Advertising and publicity	800		
5. Anything else		4,500	5.9
Parish Ministries			
1. Worship	$ 500		
2. Staff salaries	15,000		
3. Administrative supplies	2,000		
4. Leadership training	300		
5. Utilities	6,000		
6. Maintenance	2,500		
7. Travel-car allowance	2,000		
8. Benefits	2,500		
9. Insurance	3,000		
10. Contingency	1,500		
		35,300	46.3
Parish Development			
1. Property-debt reduction	$15,000		
2. Equipment	500		
		15,500	20.3
TOTAL		$76,300	100.0

Income:	
Weekly pledges	$65,000
Other offerings	7,500
Church school	1,200
Bequests and memorials	2,600
	$76,300

Step 3. Education.

With the completion of the second step, the work of the program committee, the fund-raising program swings into the third step, education. All of the statistical information on the congregation's past performance, the potential giving determined by a representative group of members, and the proposed program to fit those resources and extend the mission of the church, must be communicated. Somebody has to tell the people all about it. It is the education committee, the PR people, whose job it is now to tell the story.

And so in step three, a plan is developed and implemented to teach mission and Christian giving, to tell the people how it is and how it can be, too. Through a variety of ways and means and with the use of every available media—letters, visual aids, posters, broadsides, bulletins, speeches, one-to-one conversation—understanding and involvement in the life of the church is broadened and extended and utilized in every possible way.

Perhaps small group discussions are organized in the homes of selected members. Invitations are extended to designated groups of members. A turn-over chart or projected visual presentation is planned and given by members (or the pastor). The entire program of the church is explained—those statistics, that giving potential, the proposed program. Discussion flows freely. Questions are answered. Confidence is improved, fellowship is enhanced, inspiration abounds. Dedicated members go home from there to discuss their own plans for giving.

Or, instead of group discussions in the home, one big happy joyous congregational dinner, catered perhaps, could bring as many or more people together for an even more elaborate presentation—big charts, movies, multi-media visual projections, recorded sound programs, skits and speeches. It is all to tell the people about the church and what can be done.

Or, maybe you will find a combination of these methods useful, perhaps a dinner at the church followed by small group meetings in classrooms. Or you may want to skip the whole thing and just use the regular worship service to tell the people about it all. That way you will reach more people, probably, but you will certainly miss out on the personal touch and the fellowship that enhances the use of small groups. Get a group of church people together with a good meal, and the fellowship alone will generate substantial enthusiasm no matter what the program.

How you plan to tell your members about the program of the church is up to you, of course, and to the other leaders in your congregation. But you will certainly want to put together the best program for your circumstances, the one that will tell the most people possible just what can be done when the membership responds as it can.

Step 4. Response.

When you have pulled the facts together, developed a program proposal and told the members all about it, you are ready for the crucial moment—the all-important response.

In a full-fledged EMR program, this step is accomplished through visits to every member and the final tally of pledges so received. You may not want to make a visit every year, however; but when you do, I am convinced, in spite of all the work involved, that you will get the most consistent and generous response possible. More people will respond this way than in any other way. But it doesn't just happen.

A successful visits program requires planning, training, time and work. A few casual telephone calls to some potential volunteers won't do the trick. You have to select visitors with care. You need to train them and you need to visit them, too. No visitors should call on other members unless they have been called upon themselves. And then you will want to tell the congregation exactly what to expect from those visitors.

The day, the time, the assignments and the follow-through are crucial. Even the commissioning of visitors, the sermon and the prayer sending the visitors out: all have an important place in the program.

Commitment or Loyalty Sunday (or whatever name you give it) should be that day when visitors are sent out. If you don't plan visits, the day is used to receive pledges at the worship service. But the emphasis that day is inspiration. The membership has been told about the program and bombarded with facts and statistics. Now, the message of the Gospel, the message of love, must literally compel them to respond generously, proportionately.

Our Lord minced no words when he commanded us to follow. He never suggested an alternative to loving our neighbor, and he never, never said please. On this day the Lord demands our response. Dedicated hearts will respond in an overflowing show of gratitude, and love, and money. It is not easy and it is not always pleasant to say what the Lord expects, but on this day especially (or any day for that matter), the message is loud and clear. Christians who love their Lord will respond in gratitude and thankfulness.

Pledges made then are pledges to be kept. On a Sunday one or two weeks hence, the congregation's victory in achieving its goals is announced at the worship services. Prayers of thanksgiving and dedication are offered. Visitors are thanked and the life blood of the congregation reaches a new high in enthusiasm and commitment. It is a joyous moment for all.

Here are a commissioning service and a dedication service I have found most helpful:

ORDER FOR THE COMMISSIONING OF VISITORS FOR THE EVERY MEMBER RESPONSE

(The service follows the sermon. The pastor should make a brief, clear statement about the proposed visit, pointing out its purpose, and when and how it will be made.)

Minister: As a part of their ministry in (name of church), men and women of our congregation will be calling on you, their fellow members, during our Every Member Response. Will the following home visitors please present themselves before the altar to be commissioned for this ministry? (Names of visitors called).

Minister: Our help is in the Name of the Lord.

The People: Who made heaven and earth.

Minister: The Lord be with you.

The People: And with your spirit.

Minister: Let us pray:

O Lord Jesus Christ, who sent out your disciples to prepare the way for your coming: bless the work of your servants as they go out in your name in behalf of this parish, and grant that the seed they sow may bear fruit a hundredfold; who, with the Father and the Holy Ghost, are one God forevermore. Amen.

Almighty God, we ask you to renew the life and will of this parish, and to enable with your continuing help those who work in it to your glory and for the good of mankind; grant them a willing spirit, steadfast faith, perseverance in all good works, and bring us all at last into your eternal Kingdom; through Jesus Christ our Lord. Amen.

Minister: I now commission you as visitors in this parish, for the purpose of speaking to our members about the mission and ministry of our church, and for receiving their commitment of financial support for this work. May you go forth and return in joy, and in the knowledge that your labor is not in vain in the Lord.

Minister: And now, members of (name of the church), I ask of you that you receive these men and women with Christian friendliness and understanding. They have been set apart for this highly important service to you, this congregation, and their Lord. They are your fellow members and God's coworkers. Therefore, prepare yourselves thoughtfully, and prayerfully for their visit. And as they ask your commitment and service may you, like the Macedonian Christians, give "according to your means and beyond your means, of your own free will." Amen.

(Then the visitors return to their places and the service continues.)

ORDER FOR THE DEDICATION OF EMR PLEDGES

(The Every Member Response chairman comes forward to the Minister in the chancel, carrying the pledge cards in an offering plate or other suitable container.)

EMR Chairman: Pastor, I hereby present the pledges made by the members of our congregation as their response to God's love and to the world's need for the Gospel of our Lord Jesus Christ. By these commitments, we declare our intention to faithfully provide the money required to fulfill the plans for our church's mission and ministry in (year).

Minister: As pastor of this congregation, I hereby receive these pledges that they may be consecrated as our solemn promise to meet the challenge that God has placed before us.

Minister: The Lord be with you.

The People: And with your spirit.

Minister: Let us pray.

O everloving Father, you have blessed us more abundantly than we can fully know or appreciate. In response to your goodness, we offer these statements of our plans for giving during (year). May your Spirit continually enable us to honor these pledges, and, as we prosper, even to grow beyond these commitments in our giving. Use us for your purposes in this place. Use our offerings to send many others

where we ourselves cannot go, to work for the extension of your Kingdom throughout the world. And may the glory and praise be yours forevermore, for Jesus sake. Amen.
(The minister returns the pledge cards to the EMR chairman who then leaves the chancel.)

Step 5. Evaluation.

Step five puts the final wrap-up on the EMR program. This is an evaluation of what has been done, what could have been done better, and what should be done next time around. While the memories of the past weeks are fresh, tentative outlines should be developed for another year. The committee should now take steps to provide all pertinent data and results to the official board, who then authorizes the finance committee to put a proposed budget together. That budget, based on the congregation's response and as far as possible the listed priorities of the program committee, is presented to the congregation for their action. Once adopted, it is the program for the next year.

And so ends the intensive fund-raising campaign part of the congregation's stewardship program. But, as was pointed out previously, the work of the stewardship committee is a year-round process. So what culminated in an aggressive and exciting program of studies, plans, visits and pledges, now enters into a toned-down, but on-going effort of education, follow-through and advance planning for another year.

The EMR is an integral part of the stewardship program of the church, a very important part, but it is only a part. From here on the committee will be urging slow payers to speed up their contributions, distributing literature about the mission of the church, and generally reminding the faithful that the work of the church is never done, not even fund raising.

Stewardship is a lifelong process for the Christian. It is an all-year-round process for the church.

CHAPTER FIVE

Where All the Money Goes

Now that you've raised all that money for your church (or at least have the promise that it will be forthcoming), how do you go about planning for its use, keeping track of where it goes, and making sure you're not spending more than you're getting? Raising more money for your church is one thing; keeping it, or at least spending it for the purposes given, is yet something else.

Somehow you've got to put controls on spending so all that money isn't just thrown away or squandered. Unless you have a plan of some sort that outlines how you expect to spend your money, and have appropriate controls over cash, you will never know where it has gone or how it was used. Then all those beautiful programs you have planned may never come off.

If there is any one criticism of churches that echoes more often than any other, it is that too many churches manage their money inefficiently, loosely and haphazardly. When a church is run on faith alone, without tight business-management efficiency, no wonder there is never enough money to go around. The criticism is often justified, unfortunately, because some churches do not manage as a business enterprise would.

Maybe they shouldn't, all the way. But I am convinced that businesslike procedures are as important for efficient church management as they are for industry. Businesslike tactics may not be appropriate, but efficient business methods are.

Indeed, sound and imaginative financial management procedures are important for the church. Consider these assumptions:*

—That if churches are to carry out their mission effectively, their business affairs must be managed as skillfully as those of other organizations;

—That since churches are service-rendering rather than profit-making, their business policies and practices must differ in some respects from those of commercial enterprises, and that the differences must be identified;

—That churches have opportunities and responsibilities for practicing, teaching, and recommending business procedures that their members may use appropriately and satisfactorily in the marketplace;

—That helping people learn how to obtain and expend

*From the book *Church Budget Development* by Harry R. Page. Page 17. Copyright © 1964 by Prentice-Hall, Inc. Published by Prentice-Hall, Inc., Englewood Cliffs, N.J.

financial resources for the glory of God is a basic function of stewardship education.

Of course, not every business is run efficiently, either; but when it isn't, you can be sure that the business won't last long. Churches, on the other hand, have a way of surviving inept management. Aggressive preachers simply ask for more money and they get it. But that is certainly no excuse for inadequate controls and procedures. Those additional funds could be used more wisely.

Well-run churches (well-run financially at least) tend to have superior programs and effective community concerns. I believe that the methods of business can be used by the church. Even Jesus suggested the possibility. Consider the parable of the dishonest steward (Luke 16:1–8) as an example of how Jesus may have approved the use of good business methods for the church.

A PARABLE OF EFFICIENT BUSINESS METHODS

The parable of the dishonest steward may be one of the most misunderstood parables Jesus ever spoke. For most readers of the sixteenth chapter of Luke immediately ask: how in the world could Jesus have ever commended dishonesty as a path for discipleship? To commend that dishonest steward was to commend dishonesty. And obviously, to the Christian notion anyway, such commendation runs counter to everything Jesus ever taught or did.

Indeed, the question may well be asked why Jesus should use such an errant rascal to point out a moral. It would have been more pleasing to have had a more respectable character make the point of the parable. But then Jesus often used such questionable characters for his stories. He even associated with some of the worst reprobates imaginable—publicans, harlots, thieves, sinners of every description. Critics of Jesus have used those associations and this story to remind their followers that this Jesus was indeed merely a man and hardly much of a worthy man at that.

Yet the parable is here, and it is a tale of fascinating roguery, a rather simple story, yet a parable that makes its point dramatically, convincingly and at the point where it may hurt the most, our pocketbooks. Its message suggests that the church is often unfamiliar with efficient business methods and techniques.

It is obvious that the rascal in the story wasted his master's money. Of course he did, the parable even says so. Perhaps he went out on the town, spent his master's money on the horses, and lived it up with the women. Who knows? The point is that he wasted the money and sooner or later had to make up. For one day the master called him in, asked what was going on, and demanded an accounting.

The man may have not been taken by surprise, but at that point he was certainly a desperate man. "What shall I do," he asked, "since the master is taking the stewardship from me? I am not strong enough to dig, and I am ashamed to beg. What can I do?"

Being the schemer that he was, though, he pulled himself together, took stock of the situation, and developed the plan that in the end saved his neck. His scheme was simple, yet shrewd: he would make as many friends as he could among his master's clients. He would buy their kindness (sound familiar?), and then, when he was fired, he would simply get whatever he needed from his friends. In return for his kindness to them now, their response would be favorable to him when he later asked for help.

So, one by one, the rogue called his master's debtors to his desk. To the first he asked, "How much do you owe my master?"

"A 100 measures of oil."

"Then," said the steward, "may I suggest that you sit down quickly, take your bill, and write out 50."

To another he asked the same, "How much do you owe my master?"

"A 100 measures of wheat."

"Then," whispered the steward, "take your bill and write out 80."

You see, that steward was very accommodating to those customers and obviously gained a few friends by demanding only partial payments to clear up accounts. He then marked all those accounts paid in full.

The method in that man's madness was perfectly clear: he had guaranteed his security just when that security was justly doomed. The method was shrewd and calculating, well planned and executed. It was aboveboard and legal because he was responsible for his master's wealth. To be sure it was dishonest, dreadfully dishonest, but it was not against the law.

Then, as if to top it all, having made friends of his master's debtors, lost considerable money on his master's accounts, and generally proved himself a most dishonest rapscallion, he was reportedly commended by his master for his shrewdness. As if it weren't enough that the man had taken advantage of his stewardship responsibility, lo and behold, his master actually commended him for his shrewdness!

It is important to remember that Jesus was not commending the man's dishonesty in the parable. What the man did was dishonest. Rather, Jesus—and this is the point of the story—commended the man for his shrewdness: "For the sons of this world are wiser in their own generation than the sons of light." As a postscript Jesus might well have added: "The rogue acted with prompt foresight. If only the followers of my cause would do as much, from nobler motives and higher aims."

All of which says something, I think, as to the manner in which a church goes about the management of its resources. With ambition and zeal and foresight, the church can also plan its future more effectively. The conviction is there, the enthusiasm is evident; but all too often the plan is missing, the controls are confused and the management is inefficient. A little more shrewdness and foresight and planning is essential for the church on earth, too.

For when all the money and knowledge and strength and talents and opportunities that God has given to his children for the advancement of his kingdom are used with the prudence and skill of the dishonest steward, it is good. It is not tainted. The parable insists that these things—wealth and money and the pleasures of life—should simply be used more shrewdly and enthusiastically for the purposes of God's kingdom.

Unfortunately, though, that is not always the way it is. Our hasty and haphazard planning for tomorrow, our busyness with the details of today, our sloppy stewardship of resources, is not at all commended by our Lord. The parable speaks to our faith, to be sure, but it also speaks to the management of our churches. And the budgeting process is the beginning step toward that shrewd and careful planning for which the parable commends the dishonest steward. A businesslike approach to church management and resource allocation is a commendable objective for any congregation.

Because churches are not profit-oriented, their budgeting procedures may differ in many ways from those of commercial enterprises. Business budgets begin with sales forecasts and the cost of goods manufactured or bought to meet those goals. Labor costs, tax considerations, depreciation are all part of that business budget. Church budgets, on the other hand, do forecast available resources. But their costs are for programs and services rendered (all anticipated, of course) rather than labor costs. Aside from pastors, organists, secretaries and perhaps a few other people, labor costs are a small percentage of the total costs because volunteers do the work. And churches are not burdened with tax-planning consequences either. Even the management of churches differs from that of commercial enterprises. Ministers and volunteers direct the work of the church. Professional managers make the money for business.

Yet the church can make full use of advanced management procedures found in private business and government. And budgeting as a management tool is one of those procedures. It is a good tool for the church because it is not static nor inflexible. It is responsive (or should be) to the changing needs and goals of the church. It can relate directly to the planning, programming and control of the church.

In this book we use the terms "budget" and "budgeting" because these terms are familiar and easily understood. But because so many people tend to regard a budget as inflexible, as fixed, a rigid guide to spending only, a better phrase would be "resource programming." For that is what budgeting is all about—how to use the resources available to a church most efficiently to carry out its program. The success of a budget should not be measured by how close the year-end results come to it, but rather by the degree to which that budget helps the church to attain its objectives for being.

A business forecasts its sales, and on that basis budgets its costs. Or it anticipates its costs to meet a need and sets its product price high enough to cover those costs, plus profits. A government anticipates its needs and sets the tax rate at the level required to generate the revenue needed to cover those needs. And yet in each of these instances resources are not arbitrarily established because of needs considered necessary. There is a development of needs and matching resources, and a sequence of phases in the budgeting process that bring the two together. Needs are systematically reduced to meet realistic expectations of resources.

In much the same way, planning for spending goes on in the church budget-making process. Needs may be clearly evident, but resources must be anticipated to begin with. Attitudes toward giving must be improved, proportionate giving encouraged, and the tithe made a very specific part of the church member's giving consciousness. Budgeting is a process of planning.

Part of the businesslike approach to efficient church management involves control of spending. And control of spending (as well as planning for it) involves budgeting.

Somehow, many churches still manage to operate without a budget. They have for years and probably will for many years to come. Other churches pretend they have a budget. That is, they go about the process of setting up a budget, adopt it officially, and promptly forget about it. In many places the main purpose for putting a church budget together is no more than to agree on the pastor's pay and benefits for the new year. Other salaries—for organist, directors, custodians, etc.—may also be discussed. Any changes are noted on an extra copy of last year's budget. Other expenses are assumed to be the same as last year's budget indicates. Someone then adds up the old and new figures, and announces the budget for next year.

The treasurer, in his report, may go on to announce the year-end bank balance, total pledges made for the new year, and assure the congregation that there should be enough money again to make it through another year.

Questions: Has anyone looked at what the money went for last year? Are last year's budgets for postage and supplies and utilities reasonable again this year, considering the rise in the cost of everything? Was last year's budgeted figure really adequate to start with for salaries, benevolences, etc.?

At any rate, in many churches, budget making is simply not done, at least not in the efficient, systematic manner in which a business or college or hospital must go about the process. You may get along all right without a budget for your own personal checkbook, but that is your business (and a risky procedure, to be sure). Your church, however, needs a budget to plan its spending. Its monies have been given in trust for specific purposes. The use of that money ought to be planned efficiently and carefully.

HOW TO USE A CHURCH BUDGET

Effective church budgeting involves an understanding of several basic concepts: policy making, planning, programming and controlling. We have already noted some of these. But to put the process in clearer focus, let us consider for a moment just how these concepts can be used in your church budgeting process for a more effective flow of added dollars into your church's bank account.

Policies, of course, are nothing more than attitudes, really. But a church administration begins with a set of policies about how management is expected to handle certain matters. Policies reflect how salaries are to be paid, how debts are to be paid or incurred, how unscheduled emergencies are to be handled, how property is to be maintained. Policies should be determined, recorded, and, if desirable, published.

Planning on the other hand, is the development of the best course of action to accomplish certain objectives. Such plans, of course, must be in line with policy and reflect the overall direction of the church. Planning may be short-term (a series of choir concerts at Christmas), or it may be intermediate (a rearrangement of the Sunday church-school curriculum), or it may be long range (a new building). But whatever it is, as part of the budgeting process, it lays the blueprint for accomplishing objectives in line with overall policy.

Programming sets out the detail specifications for the plans and blueprints previously spelled out. Programs are specific agendas for doing what has been planned. It is the listing of anthems to be sung by the choir as well as the dates and places. It is a month-by-month schedule of what is to happen when that curriculum is redesigned. It is the step-by-step schedule for getting a new building put up (committee structure, fund raising, designing, financing, construction, dedication, etc.)

Controlling is the process of making sure that the concepts of policy making, planning and programming are fulfilled; that programming is done as planned according to policy. It is a process of evaluation, comparison and correction of deficiencies and discrepancies.

Budgeting is not the end all and be all of church record keeping. As noted previously, a church budget is no better than the use made of it by responsible church leaders. In fact, a budget can be quite a drag on an aggressive leader's program planning. Yet, used properly, it can be a very effective management tool, giving the leader potential programming aids.

Perhaps the greatest advantage of budgeting is its early warning system. Putting a budget together forces people to think and plan ahead. It compels earlier decisions. Financial and congregational weaknesses are discovered much sooner. Conscious effort toward attaining the objectives of the church is not lost in the detail of day-to-day operations. Church leaders can anticipate what may come, rather than be surprised when it happens, unannounced.

Furthermore, budgeting requires good and meaningful

organization. What needs to be done is carefully planned and responsibility assigned. The process reveals weaknesses in an organization, too: points up what is not getting done, eliminates duplication of effort.

A good budgeting procedure gets more people involved in planning the church's program. More people are knowledgeable and thus more interested in what is going on. Good budgeting improves cooperation, enhances harmony in the church, and offers almost everyone a chance to get involved.

A budget requires commitment. If we want cushions for the pews, the cost has to be included along with everything else we want. Ideas are translated eventually into dollars, and commitment in giving is required to meet those needs and wants.

Accountability is a very real advantage of budgeting. Every program or activity budgeted must be properly accounted for, financially. Resources are managed more effectively and church funds properly allocated with a budget. All in all, a budget forces a conservation of church resources and a meaningful allocation toward intended uses.

Furthermore, budgeting can instill confidence of the members in the leadership of the church. The capabilities and the objectives of the church are clearly laid out for all to see. Uncertainties and vague reporting are dispelled by accurate, clear and understandable reports.

Control of spending, as outlined in the budgeting process, also forces careful attention to progress in the gathering and use of resources. It helps to attain objectives.

And besides, when your church goes out to borrow money to build that new sanctuary, a history of careful preparation will be impressive to bankers. It is simply good management technique to budget carefully. And good budget practice assumes that other good financial policies are also followed. Banks are impressed.

Again, budgets are not the end all and be all of church financial record keeping. There are some limitations to the use of a church budget. For example, church budgets really will not make you any more money (you will spend more carefully, however). A budget could even cost you more trouble to put together than it is worth. And not all church budgets are successful once put together. Some don't work simply because the leadership is not committed to them. Others fail because the procedures used were faulty. Some budgets, once made, are never used. And some people expect too much out of a budget. They fail to recognize the limitations.

If accounting records are inadequate for meaningful comparison of budgets against actual costs, or if the organizational structure of the church inhibits budget review and change, of course the budget will fail. If those responsible for budget review fail to follow through with their assignments or when budgets are put together in an overwhelming quantity of detail, they are bound to be ineffective.

Remember that

—a budget is only an estimate, a plan, a projection. It is only as good as the guesses that went into putting it together.

—a budget, like a balance sheet, is good only on the day it was put together. To be effective it must be flexible, changeable, adaptable.

—approving a budget does not automatically put it into practice. Unless it is implemented, it won't work.

—a budget is only a tool. It does not replace effective management. To be successful, it must be used.

So no matter how you may have gone about the process before, it seems to me that budget making can be a very good way to make more money for your church. As I indicated before, when you have a budget, you can plan your spending, control it, monitor it and compare it. Budgeting is a businesslike procedure that will make the management of your money more effective.

A PROCEDURE FOR BUDGET PREPARATION

Actually, you started putting that budget together back in Chapter 4 as you were developing your funding program. You have some dollar costs attached to the program; and if you have followed through on a pledging program, you may have a reasonable estimate of what monies to expect. The program and the pledges are not the budget, but they will be the nucleus for your budget planning.

The program outlined what you wanted to do, the pledge results spell out what resources you may have to meet the costs of those programs. Now it is a process of putting together a program, a budget, that will spell out more precisely which programs you can pay for and which ones you will put off. A budget helps to match resources with plans without having a significant surplus one way or the other.

Traditional budget-making processes generally include a review of past expenditures and the increases or decreases required to maintain that same level of service. The budget is revised as available sums are assured or new costs are incurred. The result is the budget for the new year.

Modifications of the budget-making procedure suggest beginning with a zero balance (instead of what you spent last year) and requiring justification for every amount written into the budget. You start from zero and put together a brand new program actually. It may not end up looking too new, however, because the tendency is still to go back to last year, see what was spent then for insurance and mortgages and organ maintenance and assume the same or higher costs this year. But the idea is to start from the beginning and really build up a new budget from scratch.

You can vary the budgeting process by including the development of several budgets simultaneously—a minimum budget to meet required commitments, an advance budget to add something new, and a venture budget that goes all out to fund a program the congregation could reasonably be expected to achieve if giving came up to its real potential. The three-tier possibility is a procedure you may have used in your fund-raising program to indicate what could be done if response came up to expectations. Your budget can still be put together that way if you expect possible variations in available resources.

Budgets may also be put together by allocating all known available resources to various program requests on some formula basis. Each program area then would have its own spending plan developed for the year. Which is really no more than establishing a series of mini budgets for various categories of spending.

Here, however, is a procedure for putting a reasonable budget together for your church. Adapt it to the needs of your own congregation.

Actually, who is to put the budget together must be decided before the process begins. Responsibility for coordinating the process must be delegated. Often this responsibility is given to a committee on finance that reports directly to the official board of the church. The function of such a committee is not necessarily that of actually putting dollar amounts to programs, but someone must coordinate and plan and finally put together a final tally for consideration by the official board and the congregation. Usually it is a committee on finance.

Once responsibility has been delegated, the mechanics of the process can be implemented. You already have the program requests, which were developed some months ago for purposes of your fund raising. This is the nucleus of the next step.

What are your available resources? How much has the membership committed toward the program for the next year? In other words, the first step now is to estimate potential income. How much from pledges? How much from loose offerings? How much from other organizations of the church, from special appeals, special gifts, special services? Any endowment fund income or rental income or sales of services or goods? List them all to arrive at total resources available for use and distribution.

Next, consider the program of the church, the many classifications of expense, what you will be spending your money for. You have already put much of that together as you went through the EMR. But now you must be practical and establish programs based on a realistic anticipation of resources.

Is the proposed compensation for the pastor and other staff persons realistic in light of the congregation's response and their assigned responsibilities? (Read over the last chapter in this book to figure out how you should go about listing all the parts of your pastor's pay package.) Note carefully the distinction between what is compensation and what is reimbursement of professional expenses. The one is listed as part of salaries; the other is part of administration or transportation costs.

The congregation's benevolence commitments and payments to other charities need to be considered carefully. These make up the outreach program of the church. The outreach program is an important part of the total costs of the church; yet it is the one part easiest to cut in favor of other, more pressing needs. It may also be the budget item least understood by the membership simply because it is money that goes out to other programs away from the church. Support of the outreach program will depend upon the commitment of the pastor and the congregation to it.

The religious education needs of the parish are fully as important as any others. Costs for supplies, facilities, textbooks, visual aids and sundry other items can be important. Not only is the past record of expenditures significant, but future plans become increasingly important as other attractions make inroads on participation by youth and adults alike in the life of the church.

Maintenance of the church properties is no small budget item. A subsequent chapter discusses ways to keep those costs within reason. But certainly a church plant must be maintained and insured or it will eventually collapse. Besides, an attractive building can be an asset to the congregation, not only in dollars and cents, but also as good public relations.

There is little you can do about debt retirement at this point. With commitments already made, you will just total in what is due for the year. Of course, when new commitments are anticipated, considerable attention should be given to the impact of that cost on subsequent budgets. If resources are available now, prepayments on existing indebtedness could be considered.

The actual program of the church is tied up with the promotional activities of the church. Here is public relations, advertising, stewardship, music supplies, office maintenance and all the other costs associated with plans and programs and administration.

The total of the dollars attached to all the items of expense make up the total picture. That is your budget. And unless you put it together in a format that will help you to plan and control, you will be spending far more money than you should without accomplishing your objectives effectively. There is more money for your church in a budget because you know what you have or will spend. Cutting off the spigot and diverting monies somewhere else (or not at all) is done successfully only if you know where you have been and where you are headed. In part, that is what a budget is for.

A budget worksheet can be a very simple document. The first column may be no more than a listing by categories of all the needs of the church. You have already spelled this out in the development of the program for your EMR. (See your Parish Program Proposal.) Your worksheet will include a second column of actual costs for existing programs for the past and/or current year. Finally, in a third column a realistic budget is put together based on anticipated resources. Thus, a simple budget is three columns on a worksheet.

A more elaborate arrangement could be much more useful to you, once you have all your committee requests for funds in hand. It could also be more confusing. But consider these possibilities for a nine columnar worksheet:

Column #	Item
1.	Item
2.	Cost: last full year
3.	Cost: this year–9 months
4.	Cost: this year–3 months estimated
5.	Cost: this year estimated
6.	Program needs next year
7.	Minimum budget next year
8.	Advance budget next year
9.	Probable budget following year

You can fill in the columns and on the basis of past experience mathematically determine what your budget ought to be for next year and even the next. Naturally some hard decisions will be required when resources do not meet even minimum budget needs. A past record of costs may be helpful therefore in anticipating trends in the cost of fixed items, such as utilities and insurance. And some projections into the following year will help you to anticipate at an early date needs fòr that time, assuming few changes in current programming.

Making the budget doesn't just happen one day when the committee chairman and the pastor sit down over a cup of coffee to talk about next year's plans. It is an ongoing process that requires a heavy concentration of time toward the end of the fiscal year and also time during the rest of the year for planning, evaluation and review. I have outlined the possibilities for you.

CASH FLOW PLAN

One final and important item in budget preparation is a cash flow plan. Indeed, have a good cash flow plan and you can literally add dollars to your church resources.

The in-flow of funds into a church treasury is seasonal. There is a huge swell at Christmas and Easter and a rather drastic drop in the summer, we all know that. It has probably always been that way and I don't see much chance for a change in spite of repeated pleas from church leaders for a change. Expenses do go on all year, even in the summer, but offerings just don't come in evenly.

Consequently, some churches will have more cash than they need in December and April, and most congregations will not have enough in the summer. But just to know that is the case is not enough. How much too much and how much too little when known reasonably well, can be used to advantage to add interest income or cut interest costs. Surplus funds can be invested, but only a cash flow worksheet can reasonably anticipate for just how long. Some expendi-

CASH FLOW WORKSHEET

	Jan	Feb	Mar	Apr	May	June	July	Aug	Sept	Oct	Nov	Dec
Anticipated Offerings:	$2,000	$1,900	$1,900	$2,500	$2,000	$1,600	$1,200	$1,500	$1,600	$1,800	$2,200	$3,000
Budgeted Expenses:												
Benevolences	400	400	400	400	400	400	400	400	400	400	400	400
Salaries	600	600	600	600	600	600	600	600	600	600	600	600
Debt	500	500	500	500	500	500	500	500	500	500	500	500
Insurance	–0–	–0–	–0–	–0–	–0–	–0–	–0–	–0–	1200	–0–	–0–	–0–
Utilities	200	300	200	150	150	100	75	75	100	100	150	200
Miscellaneous	200	100	200	300	200	100	150	250	200	200	100	100
	1,900	1,900	1,900	1,950	1,850	1,700	1,725	1,825	3,000	1,800	1,750	1,800
Cash Surplus/ (Deficit)	100	–0–	–0–	550	150	(100)	(525)	(325)	(1,400)	–0–	450	1,200
Accumulated Cash Surplus/ (Deficit)	100	100	100	650	800	700	175	(150)	(1,550)	(1,550)	(1,100)	100

tures could be deferred during the summer months, but only a cash flow projection will tell you which ones and for how long.

The first step then is to spread that budget (income and expenses) out over all twelve months of the year according to the months in which the amounts will be spent. Look at the illustration.

By taking that estimated cash balance figure and attempting to balance it out more evenly with a rearrangement of expense payments, you will need to borrow less cash to make up the summer deficit (thus cutting interest costs) and be able to take advantage of all the discounts you have coming. Likewise, surplus cash can be invested and you will know for how long.

Furthermore, a periodic forecasting of the financial condition of the church helps to update the cash flow report as well as to estimate how things are going now and are expected to go in the short-range.

A careful use of the cash flow budget is an extremely important procedure for anticipating cash needs. It too is part of the process of trying to get more money for your Church.

CHAPTER SIX

Telling It Like It Is

One of the most effective ways of getting more money for your church is to keep the membership informed about what is going on. When people know what is going on, they are more likely to respond, somehow. Of course, a good response from church members will often depend on their being told good things. But even bad news can be approached with a positive attitude and a resulting generous response.

The key, however, to telling the members how things are is a good system of records coupled with honest, factual reports. An accounting system that accurately records the facts in a simple, easy-to-use way is particularly important for pulling together quickly all the facts required for informative reporting.

And that is what this chapter is all about: how to keep

financial records and how to report the results. Do it right, and there is a good chance the Sunday offering count may show a good gain.

INTERNAL CONTROL*

A system of accounting and reporting for the management of the finances of any church begins not with the checkbook or the cash disbursements journal, but with the development of a good system of internal control.

Adequate internal checks on the assets of your church are extremely important; yet in too many churches, this checking is ignored altogether or is at best carelessly planned. Control features may be missing in your church simply because your congregation has failed to agree upon and follow generally accepted accounting principles for the management of its cash and other assets. Responsible congregational leaders, just as responsible businessmen, must establish appropriate internal control safeguards if their stewardship of the church's resources is not to be questioned.

But what is internal control? Just this. It is a plan of control, not only to detect error or fraud, but to safeguard assets; to check the accuracy and dependability of financial records and reports; to encourage operating efficiency and adherence to rules, regulations and policies set by management. In a sense, internal control is thus the very basis on which the accounting system of the church is established.

Many churches, nevertheless, ignore the pleas of those who urge better internal control and accounting procedures. Objections are raised on the presumption that church mem-

---

**Church and Clergy Finance,* Vol. 4, No. 2, Ministers Life Resources, Minneapolis, Minn. (March, 1973). Used with permission.

bers are above reproach; and thus normal procedures to check on suspicious employees, or to remove temptations for weaker employees, are out of place in the church. Yet churches are vulnerable to fraud and theft, too.

Cases can be cited of significant losses incurred due to insufficient control and questionably loyal treasurers. Mismanagement is not new to congregations. Good internal control procedures reduce the possibilities for misappropriation and afford protection to congregational leaders in the stewardship of members' contributions entrusted to their care.

Your congregation's internal control system can be greatly improved by accepting and implementing certain specific procedures. Here are some suggestions.

1. Different persons should count the offering, write checks, keep the individual contributions records and reconcile the bank statements. Separation of duties in this way greatly reduces the chances for misappropriation of funds and for error. The responsibilities might be divided this way: the financial secretary records individual contributions; the treasurer writes all checks; the chairman of the finance committee reconciles the bank statements; and the head ushers assume responsibility for counting the offerings and reporting the results and bank deposits to the financial secretary and treasurer.

2. At least two people should be in custody of the offering until it is deposited in a bank or placed in a night depository or safe.

3. Offerings and all contributions received during the week should be deposited as soon as possible, the same way as for the Sunday offerings. The less time offerings remain in the church, the less opportunity for loss from theft, fire, etc.

4. Offering envelopes should be distributed and used by all members. Reports should be made periodically of con-

tributions. Any discrepancies should be reported immediately. This kind of check on a member's contributions makes certain offerings are actually received and deposited to the use of the congregation.

5. Members should be encouraged to write checks rather than use cash even with an envelope system. Checks are less negotiable than cash and also provide a receipt and record for the donor.

6. Access to offerings should be limited to the head ushers. Access to the bank account should be limited to the treasurer.

7. Bank statements should not be reviewed by the treasurer, but should be received by the finance committee chairman and reconciled promptly by him from information provided by the treasurer. Substantiating documents should accompany all check requests and payments and should be cancelled, once paid, to avoid reuse as a substantiating document.

8. All checks should be signed by the treasurer, or by him and one other person. The pastor should have no access to the bank account simply for his own protection. These restrictions place control and responsibility for all disbursements with the treasurer.

9. All payments should be by check. A check protector is useful. Accounting for all disbursements is easy with prenumbered checks. Imprinted, personalized checks are desirable.

10. The church budget should be the basis for all expenditures. Any variations should be explained, yet some flexibility is necessary. Expenditure control is virtually impossible without budget guidelines. Thus, the church budget is a very important internal control document.

11. An audit should be conducted annually, either by a qualified audit committee or an outside auditor.

12. All cash handling procedures should be in writing.

As financial officers change, it is important to continue consistent record keeping and reporting procedures. A written record provides the documentation and instruction for new volunteers.

13. A fidelity bond should be secured to cover those persons responsible for church finances. Some denominations provide this coverage to all congregational leaders; most do not, however. Your congregation's insurance advisor can suggest necessary coverage.

Even if your congregation has operated smoothly and without difficulty all these years, it is still important to initiate internal control procedures now. Responsible stewardship, operating efficiency, accuracy and reliability of your records and reports, is vastly improved with proper internal control. Even St. Paul suggested (2 Cor. 8:20–21) that those who handle gifts do so properly so as "not to stir up any complaints about the way we handle this generous gift. Our purpose is to do what is right, not only in the sight of the Lord, but also in the sight of men."

What is proper may be neither the easiest way nor the way you do things now, but it is the best way.

AN ACCOUNTING SYSTEM

There may be as many different accounting systems for churches as there are churches. At least, there is no standard accounting system used by very many congregations. In fact, few books even offer specific systems on church accounting.* And there is as yet no one standard volume describing typical systems adaptable to congregations of varying size.

---

*However, see my book *Accounting Methods for the Small Church.* (*See* bibliography).

On the next several pages, however, is a brief yet complete system especially useful to smaller congregations but easily adaptable to the needs of larger congregations, also. It is a proven method, simple to use, easy to keep, and with useful reports as an end product.

This system bypasses the traditional use of ledgers. Instead, it makes use of the typical cash receipts and cash disbursements journal; and it is a double-entry bookkeeping system (an important feature, incidentally, for accurate transaction recording). The step-by-step instructions should be particularly useful to the many nonaccountants who are church treasurers. In short, it is really a fool-proof system almost any church treasurer can use. Adapt it to your own needs and you may be surprised at how well it serves the purposes of your congregation.

INSTRUCTIONS FOR USING CHURCH ACCOUNTING SYSTEMS

REPORT Number 1: Counters' Report of Cash Receipts and Weekly Analysis of Deposits

1. Immediately following each worship service sort all envelopes, loose offerings, church school offerings and any other offerings into separate piles.

2. Count the money in each envelope, making certain the amount enclosed is correctly marked on the outside. Enter coins, bills and checks in envelopes in column 1, lines 5 to 9.

3. If the loose offering includes checks without envelopes, the check should be handled as though received in an envelope. Place with it a slip of paper properly marked with the name of the payer, the amount of the check and the purpose of the offering. Enter the amounts of coins and bills received in loose offering in column 2, lines 5 and 6.

4. Enter the amount of coins, bills and checks received in the church school offering and other special offerings in appropriate columns on lines 5 to 9.

5. The total of coins, bills and checks listed in column 6, lines 5 to 9, must be the same as that listed on the deposit slip.

6. Sometime after the offering is deposited, sort and tabulate the envelopes. Enter the proper amounts on lines 17 to 35. The total amount of money deposited and shown on line 9, column 6, must be the same as the total offering recorded on line 35, column 6.

7. Transfer the totals on line 35 to Report 2, lines 1 to 10, for the proper week of the month.

REPORT Number 2: Monthly Report of Offerings

1. Complete columns 1 to 6, lines 1 to 10, for the month. Information for the respective weekly tabulations of offerings are on Report 1. The total of column 6 must be the same as the total deposits for the month.

2. Copy column 6, lines 1 to 10 onto lines 25 to 33 in column 1 and also onto Report 4, column 2, lines 1 to 11.

3. Copy last month's Report 2, column 3, lines 25 to 33 onto this month's report 2, column 2, lines 25 to 33. Enter totals of each line in column 3.

4. Copy column 3, lines 25 to 33 onto Report 4, column 2, lines 21 to 32 and also onto next month's Report 2, column 2, lines 25 to 33.

CASH DISBURSEMENTS JOURNAL (Complete this Journal before doing Report 3)

1. From information in the checkbook, list in numerical order all checks written during the month. Distribute the correct amounts in the appropriate expense columns.

2. At the end of the month, total all columns.

3. The sum of the totals of columns 1 to 5 must equal the sum of the totals of columns 6 to 25. (Columns 2 to 5 may have plus or minus or zero balances.)

4. Enter the sum of columns 2 to 5, line 36 in Report 4, column 3, line 12.

5. Enter the sum of columns 2 to 5, line 38, in Report 4, column 3, line 33 and column 4, lines 12 and 33.

6. Enter the totals of columns 6 to 24, lines 36 and 38, on the appropriate lines on Report 3, columns 4 and 5, respectively.

7. The sum of columns 6 to 24, lines 36 and 38, must be the same as line 41 on Report 3, columns 4 and 5, respectively.

8. Enter detail of column 25, lines 36 and 38, in Report 4, column 3, lines 5 to 10 and 26 to 31 respectively.

9. Column 1, lines 36 and 38 of the Cash Disbursements Journal must be the same as Report 4, column 3, lines 16 and 37, respectively, for this bank account.

REPORT Number 3: Statement of Expenditures

1. Columns 1, 2 and 3 may be completed at any convenient time from information in the annual budget.

2. Columns 4 and 5 are to be completed from information in columns 6 to 24 of the Cash Disbursements Journal. Certain detailed analysis of columnar totals in the Cash Disbursements Journal may be necessary to provide the information required on Report 3. Total salaries, for instance, in column 7 of the Journal must be divided on Report 3 among pastor, office, music and others.

3. The totals of columns 4 and 5 on lines 5 and 40 should be copied onto Report 4, column 3, lines 3 and 4 and lines 24 and 25.

REPORT Number 4: Statement of Fund Receipts, Disbursements and Balances; and Statement of Bank Account Changes

A. Fund receipts, lines 1 to 13 and 21 to 32

1. Column 1, lines 1 to 13 and 21 to 32 are a repeat of the same lines from columns 4 and 1, respectively, of last month's report.

2. Amounts in column 2, lines 1 to 19 are copied from Report 2, column 1, lines 25 to 33. Lines 21 to 32 are from Report 2, column 3, lines 25 to 33.

3. Amounts in column 3, lines 3 and 4 and lines 24 and 25 are from Report 3, columns 4 and 5, lines 5 and 40.

4. On each line, add columns 1 and 2, deduct column 3, to determine the amount for column 4, which will be the balance in each fund and in each checking account.

B. Bank account changes, lines 15 to 19 and 36 to 40

1. Column 1, lines 15 to 19 are the same as lines 15 to 19 of column 4 last month. Column 1, lines 36 to 40 are the same as lines 36 to 40 in column 1 of last month's report.

2. Column 2 includes all deposits made during the month or year in each bank account, the same as line 33, columns 1 and 3, Report 2.

3. Column 3 includes the total of all checks written during the month or year on each bank account as recorded in the Cash Disbursements Journal, column 1, lines 36 and 38.

4. Column 4, lines 13, 19, 34 and 40 are the reconciled bank balances (see Report 5) at the end of the month and must all be the same. Lines 1 to 19 must be identical to lines 22 to 40.

C. Payroll deductions, lines 12 and 33

1. For column 1, lines 12 and 33: repeat the information from last month's report, column 4.

2. For column 3, line 12: if payroll deductions exceed cash payments during the month, then deduct the sum of columns 3, 4 and 5, line 36 of the Cash Disbursements Journal; if not, add the sum.

3. For column 3, line 33: if payroll deductions exceed cash payments for the year to date, then deduct the sum of columns 3, 4 and 5, line 38 of the Cash Disbursements Journal; if not, add the sum.

4. For column 4, lines 12 and 33: do the opposite done for column 3, line 33.

Individual Contributions Record

One further bit of record keeping you will need to develop is a system for keeping track of all the contributions from members—an individual contributions record system. Here again, there is a wide assortment of possible systems. Any church offering-envelope manufacturing firm will have a plan. Your own church denominational publishing house will, too.

The illustrated form in this chapter has proved useful to me. It is to be hand-kept, and could become burdensome in large congregations. But as congregations grow, machine systems, even a computer, become necessary. Nevertheless, even the form illustrated here could be adapted for machine or computer use when that time comes for your congregation.

A SYSTEM FOR REPORTING

With all the information collected through an accounting system, the next step is to put it on an appropriate form for reporting. It is important to keep the financial records carefully; but it is equally important to report the results.

The frequency and nature of such reporting can make it an effective money raiser for your church.

In those churches where reports on individual giving are mailed out immediately following the last Sunday of the month, the offering for the first Sunday of the next month is always the largest. The monthly report is not only a reminder of giving response thus far and the total commitments made, but it is a record of the member's giving for his personal use as well. Most members appreciate the information.

Congregations that report less frequently are missing an excellent opportunity to get more money for their church. For it can easily be shown that a reminder or a report prompts a response. Wait until December 31 to mail out that report and you have missed a chance to raise a few extra dollars. The impact of that reminder is lost because the incentive to give is gone—the year is over, the books are closed, and besides, even the tax advantage is gone, too.

Creative monthly reporting can generate a significant response. Try using the samples on the next few pages to test the idea on your congregation. Of course, you will need to adapt the information to your own church. But telling the members of the congregation more than just what they gave gives you an opportunity to educate them in missions or church administration or benevolences or debt retirement. A dry report or a carbon copy of a form is not very creative. It will generate some response, maybe. Add some imagination to the idea, though, and you may be in for some long-term pleasant surprises.

Creative development of the annual report is important, too, for telling the congregation where you have been. It will help to set sights for the new year even if offerings will no longer be credited to last year. Missed opportunities and neglected programs can be pointed up in the annual report as a means of creating interest in giving more. And healthy attitudes of stewardship can be promoted to advantage.

Year

Month

Day

COUNTERS' REPORT OF CASH RECEIPTS

REPORT NO. 1

	1	2	3	4	5	6
WEEKLY CASH COUNT OF OFFERINGS						
	Envelopes	Loose	Church School	Other	Other	Deposit
Coins						
Bills						
Checks						
TOTAL						
WEEKLY ANALYSIS OF DEPOSITS						
	Benevolences	Current	Other	Other	Other	Total
Envelopes:						
Benevolences						
Current						
Others (List):						
Total Envelopes						
Loose						
Church School						
Others (List):						
TOTAL						

Year ________

MONTHLY REPORT OF OFFERINGS

Month ________

REPORT NO. 2

	1	2	3	4	5	6
	First Week	Second Week	Third Week	Fourth Week	Fifth Week	Total Monthly Deposit
THIS MONTH						
Benevolences						
Current						
Other						
Other						
Other						
TOTAL DEPOSITS						
YEAR TO DATE						
	Total This Month	Year to Date Last Month	Year to Date This Month			
Benevolences						
Current						
Other						
Other						
Other						
TOTAL DEPOSITS						

YEAR______ MONTH_____

CASH DISBURSEMENTS JOURNAL

Name of Bank__________________

	Payee	1 Amount of check	2 Income Tax Withheld	3 Social Security Tax W/H	4 City or State Tax W/H	5 Other With-holdings	6 Benevo-lences	7 Salaries & allow-ances
1								
2								
3								
4								
5								
6								
7								
8								
9								
10								
11								
12								
13								
14								
15								
16								
17								
18								
19								
20								
21								
22								
23								
24								
25								
26								
27								
28								
29								
30								
31								
32								
33								
34								
35								
36	TOTAL THIS MONTH							
37	PRIOR MO. YR-TO-DATE							
38	TOTAL YEAR-TO-DATE							
39								
40								

8	9	10	11	12	13	14	15	16
Pulpit Supply, Substitutes	Taxes Pension Etc.	Office Supplies Postage	Miscel- laneous	Transfers	Worship, Music Bulletins	Christian Education SCS,VCS	Steward- ship, Evangelism	Youth Activities

17 Social Ministry	18 Parsonage Loan & Interest	19 Parsonage Utilities Taxes, Ins.	20 Parsonage Mntc., & Repair	21 Church Loan & Interest	22 Church Utilities Taxes, Ins.	23 Church Mntc.,& Repair	24 Other Items	25 Other Funds	
									1
									2
									3
									4
									5
									6
									7
									8
									9
									10
									11
									12
									13
									14
									15
									16
									17
									18
									19
									20
									21
									22
									23
									24
									25
									26
									27
									28
									29
									30
									31
									32
									33
									34
									35
									36
									37
									38
									39
									40

YEAR ____________

MONTH ____________

STATEMENT OF EXPENDITURES

REPORT NUMBER THREE

	1 Budget for Year	2 Budget for Month	3 Budget to Date	4 Actual for Month	5 Actual for Year	6
BENEVOLENCES						
District-Conference						
Other						
Total						
CURRENT OPERATIONS						
General Adm.						
Salaries and Allowances — Pastor						
Office						
Music						
Other						
Pulpit Supply						
Taxes, Pensions						
Office Supplies						
Miscellaneous						
Transfers						
Total						
Parish Adm.						
Worship, Music						
Christian Ed;						
Stew., Ev.,						
Youth Activities,						
Social Ministry						
Total						
Property Adm.						
Parsonage — Loan & Int.						
Util., Taxes						
Maint.						
Church — Loan & Int.						
Util., Taxes						
Maint.						
Total						
Total Current						
BENEV. & CURRENT						

STATEMENT OF FUND RECEIPTS, DISBURSEMENTS AND BALANCES and BANK ACCOUNT CHANGES REPORT NUMBER FOUR	① Beginning Cash Balances	② Receipts	③ Disbursements	④ Ending Cash Balances
THIS MONTH				
FUNDS				
Benevolence				
Current				
Other				
Other				
Other				
Total				
Payroll Deductions				
Total				
BANK ACCOUNTS (List)				
Total				
YEAR TO DATE				
FUNDS				
Benevolence				
Current				
Other				
Other				
Other				
Total				
Payroll Deductions				
Total				
BANK ACCOUNTS (List)				

BANK RECONCILIATION

Name of Bank ______________________

YEAR ______
MONTH ______
DATE ______

REPORT NUMBER FIVE

Balance shown on bank statement

Add: Deposits made but not appearing on bank statements

Deduct: Checks which do not yet appear on the bank statement

List: Ck. number

Adjusted bank balance

Balance shown on check book

Add: Deposits not yet recorded in check book or on Reports No. 1 or No. 2

Less: Charges appearing on bank statement but not yet recorded in Cash Disbursements Journal

Adjusted check book balance

NOTE: Lines 19 and 35 must be the same. They must also be the same as lines 16 and 37, Column 4, Report Number 4 for this bank account.

EMPLOYEE PAYROLL RECORD

NAME

ADDRESS

SOCIAL SECURITY NUMBER

	Date	1 Gross Salary	2 Income Tax Withheld	3 Social Security Tax	4	5	6 Net Amount of Check
1							
2							
3							
4							
5							
6							
7							
8							
9							
10							
11							
12							
13							
14	Quarterly Total						
15							
16							
17							
18							
19							
20							
21							
22							
23							
24							
25							
26							
27							
28							
29	Quarterly Total						
30							
31							
32							
33	Total to Date						
34							
35							
36							
37							
38							
39							
40							

INDIVIDUAL CONTRIBUTOR'S RECORD

Name____ No. ____________

Address____

Phone____

Year	Sun	First Quarter			Second Quarter			Third Quarter			Fourth Quarter		
Pledged Given		Jan.	Feb.	Mar.	April	May	June	July	Aug.	Sept.	Oct.	Nov.	Dec.
Current Pledge/wk.	1												
$______ Given:/qrt.	2												
1______	3												
2______	4												
3______ 4______	5												
T______	T												
Benevolence Pledge/wk.	1												
$______ Given:/qrt.	2												
1______	3												
2______	4												
3______ 4______	5												
T______	T												
Building Fund Pledge/wk.	1												
$______ Given:/qrt.	2												
1______	3												
2______	4												
3______ 4______	5												
T______	T												
Special Offerings	1												
Given:/qrt.	2												
1______	3												
2______ 3______	4												
4______	5												
T______	T												

SAMPLES OF MONTHLY REPORTING

ST. TIMOTHY CHURCH
Chicago, Illinois
January 19__

ONE MONTH AGO . . . the new year began and with it you began using a new set of church offering envelopes. Many of you in the new year were inspired to greater visions of giving through your recent pledge for the current and benevolence funds of St. Timothy Church.

ONE MONTH AGO . . . your church treasurer started a new church accounting year. He reports the following expenditures for January:

Benevolences	$ 000
Pastoral ministry	000
Programming	000
Maintenance	000
Debt retirement	000
	$0000

ONE MONTH AGO . . . your financial secretary also opened a new ledger sheet for you. He reports that for the month of January you gave:

$______ to current and benevolence funds

$______ to the building fund

(If incorrect, call 399-0540)

. . . . He also reports that you have pledged for 19__

$_____ to current and benevolence funds per week.

$_____ to the building fund per week.

. . . . And he reports that total offerings in January were $0,000 for current and benevolence funds, and $000 for the building fund.

ONE MONTH IS GONE . Have *you* gone one-twelfth of the way to meet your promised gift to God in 19__? You promised your loyalty to Jesus Christ in all things. Have you *been* loyal to him in *all* things?

ST. JOHN CHURCH
New York
March 19__

DO YOU HELP TO SUPPORT WORLD MISSIONS?

Yes! when you contribute to your Lord through St. John Church. And you help to support many other worthwhile causes, too, through your generous gifts to benevolences.

FOR EXAMPLE . . . BY YOUR GIVING

You help to establish and maintain mission congregations such as ours throughout the nation.

You help refugees who call a cave or a rooftop their home, who gratefully wear your old clothes until they literally fall off.

You help orphaned children, unwed mothers, aged men and women through your gifts to our own welfare society.

You help support the colleges and seminaries of our church where your children will have the opportunity for a Christian education, where pastors may be trained to serve your congregation.

And you help hundreds more . . . WHEN you contribute to your church!

ACCORDING to the records of our financial secretary, you *did* help during March. Of our total monthly offering of $0000 for current and benevolence funds, and $000 for the building fund, you gave:

$______ for current and benevolence funds
$______ for the building fund
(If incorrect, call 399-0540)

MANY will certainly thank you for your generous gift!

YOU MAY BE INTERESTED to know that during March the following expenditures were made:

Benevolences	$ 000
Pastoral ministry	000
Programming	000
Maintenance	000
Debt retirement	000
	$0,000

CHRIST CHURCH
Toledo, Ohio
May 19__

WHAT ARE "OFFICE SUPPLIES AND MISCELLANEOUS?"

. . . perhaps you would like to know!

The annual budget of Christ Church includes several groups of expenditures. One of these groups is labeled MAINTENANCE. This includes office supplies, postage, *The Parish,* church building maintenance, utilities and miscellaneous.

The Parish cost includes the expenses necessary to send this weekly magazine into every one of our homes.

Church-building maintenance and expenses are those necessary to repair, maintain, or otherwise keep the church building in good physical order. Utilities include gas, electricity, water and phone.

Office supplies and postage are such items as are necessary to promote the work of the church. They include:

. . . this paper you hold in your hands.
. . . the ink used to mimeograph this letter.
. . . the stencil used to produce the letter.
. . . the envelope used to mail it to you.
. . . the postage paid to send the letter to you.

Miscellaneous expenditures are those that do not conveniently fit into any other category: Sunday bulletins, lists of new families moving into the community, a surprise gift for the minister.

YES, IT COSTS MONEY TO OPERATE A CHURCH . . . and you have helped to keep it going through your weekly contributions to Christ Church.

ACCORDING to the records of the financial secretary (if incorrect, please call 399-0540), you have given the following amounts for the work of the church during May:

$_____ to the current and benevolence funds
$_____ to the building fund

TOTAL OFFERINGS in May were: $0,000 for current and benevolence
$ 000 for the building fund

CALVARY CHURCH
Miami, Florida
June 19__

HALFWAY THERE? . . .

Here is the record. Decide for yourself!

Budget for January through June $0,000

Total offerings to the current and benevolence funds, six months $0,000

Total actual expenditures January through June $0,000

YOUR SHARE . . .

You wanted to give:

$______ to the current and benevolence funds for six months

$______ to the building fund for six months

You did give:

$______ to the current and benevolence funds, January–June

$______ to the building fund, January–June

(If incorrect, please call 399-0540)

HALFWAY THERE? . . .

This is the record. Decide for yourself!

Total offerings for June were: $0,000 to the current and benevolence funds
$ 000 to the building fund

Total expenditures for June were: $ 000 Benevolences
000 Pastoral ministry
000 Programming
000 Maintenance
000 Debt retirement
$0,000

SALEM CHURCH
Portland, Oregon
September, 19__

HOW MUCH DO I HAVE TO GIVE TO THE CHURCH? . . . . *nothing!*
GIVING IS A PERSONAL THING

And you give because . . .

–you want to give because of what Christ has done for you.

–you need to give for the same reason (and not because the church necessarily needs your gift.)

YOU SHOULD GIVE:

–NOW, not when you can afford to give. If you waited until you could afford to buy a car, or afford to raise a family, or afford to give, you would never buy a car, or never have a family, or never give.

–PROPORTIONATELY, a definite percentage: 5, 10 or 15 percent, or more!

–REGULARLY, every week.

–MORE, because we never give enough. Jesus Christ demands our whole life.

In September you did give for the work of the church:

$______ to current and benevolence funds

$______ to the building fund

(If incorrect, please call 399-0540)

WHAT PERCENTAGE OF YOUR MONTHLY INCOME WAS THAT?—a little or a whole lot? "God so loved the world that HE GAVE his only begotten Son, that whosoever believeth in him should not perish, but have everlasting life." John 3:16.

Total offerings in September were: $0,000 for the current and benevolence funds

$ 000 for the building fund

Total expenditures were:	Benevolences	$ 000
	Pastoral ministry	000

Programming	000
Maintenance	000
Debt retirement	000
	$0,000

THE ANNUAL AUDIT

An audit won't necessarily get your church any more money at all. In fact, it might even cost you some money. But a church financial management system is incomplete without this annual check-up on the past year's finances.

In fact, every congregation ought to have an annual audit as part of its financial record-keeping procedures. It may even be required if your congregation carries fidelity bond insurance. Many denominations insist on annual audit reports along with statistical data. Besides, your bank will require an audited financial statement if you seek funds for a capital improvements project.

Adequate audits assure members that their contributions have been used for intended purposes, that the treasurer has handled financial transactions satisfactorily, that a new treasurer will start with accurate records, that legal and official forms have been properly completed and that the church's financial picture is as the statements say it is.

The finance committee is normally responsible for the audit. It may appoint an audit committee either to do the actual audit or to supervise the work of others. Its responsibilities for the audit would include examining and reviewing all records and accounts; examining and inspecting all insurance policies, records of securities, real estate records, inventories and records of other investments; preparing necessary schedules and reports; and recommending changes or suggestions for improvement to the finance committee.

Specific auditing procedures include the following steps:

1. Cash receipts—

Your committee will need to review the methods for handling monies received from worship service offerings as well as in the mails, trace the amounts so received to the cash receipts journal, compare the entries in the journal with the duplicate deposit slips, and examine the transaction record for proper account classification.

The audit committee will also trace the deposits from the counter's reports to the journal and compare these entries with the deposits actually recorded by the bank. At the same time, it will check the timeliness of the deposit, check the account distribution in the cash receipts journal and check the use of the money received for specific purposes to make sure it got into the proper fund.

2. Cash expenditures—

All cash disbursements (checks or cash) must be recorded in the cash disbursements journal showing the date, check number, the name of the payee, the amount of the check and the distribution to the proper account classification.

Then, the audit committee must test-check the bookkeeping entries in the journal for proper recording in the appropriate class of expenditure.

The committee will also foot (add) the journal for accounting accuracy; examine the authority for writing a check; the authority for approving the payment of invoices, the records of a minister's call, including the current salary and housing arrangements; the adequacy of contract agreements; the action of the official board in their minutes; and verify that the checks written for expenses were actually paid to the proper parties.

If prenumbered checks are used (and they should be), the committee must account for all checks used. If the treasurer has not already done so, the committee should prepare a statement of expenditures for comparison with the adopted budget for the year, as well as analyze expenditures for major improvements, refurbishings and new equipment for addition to asset accounts.

3. Bank statement reconciliation—

The audit committee, rather than some other group or individual, should prepare the year-ending reconciliation between the bank balance and the balance shown on the books.

The reconciliation begins with the bank balance, to which is added deposits shown on the books but not yet credited on the bank statement. Outstanding checks are then subtracted to prove the book balance.

In the process of preparing the reconciliation, the committee must also verify on a test-check basis that proper endorsements are on the cancelled checks.

Furthermore, a request to the bank to confirm by direct written confirmation the balances held in the commercial and/or savings accounts is a normal and important procedure. An inspection of bank signature cards for approved signatures will make certain proper people are writing the checks.

4. Petty cash funds—

Petty cash funds are difficult to control. Thus proper checks by the committee are important. The committee must determine that disbursement vouchers have proper approval, that reimbursements to the fund are made properly, that maximum figures for individual payments have been established and that there is adequate approval for advances to employees and for I.O.U.s.

5. Individual member contributions records—

The committee should compare "pledged amounts" with

signed pledges, if any. A test-check of the financial secretary's posting of contributions to the members' records will verify accuracy.

6. Insurance policies—

A check of all church insurance in force should be made. A schedule of coverages can be completed by the committee to show effective and expiration dates, kind and classification of coverages, maximum amounts of each coverage, premium amounts and terms of payment. If there is an insurance appraisal, it should be compared with actual insurance coverage.

7. Amortization of debt—

The committee must verify balances owing to all lenders by a direct confirmation, in writing. It must also review the terms of the loans and prepare a schedule of delinquencies, if any.

8. Securities and other investments—

The committee must count all securities by the identifying number on certificates or accounts and then prepare a schedule listing the numbers and amounts for each security. The committee must also make certain that all securities are in the name of the church. It will also set forth the pertinent facts concerning other investments such as notes, mortgages and real estate.

Of course, there is not much point in having an audit if the internal control procedures of the church are weak or inadequate. As noted at the beginning of this chapter, you have potential problems if only one person is counting the offering, or one person approves expenditures and writes the checks to pay those bills, or church offerings are deposited in some other account rather than in the church's name, or only one signature is included on the bank authorization card, or checks are presigned, or the same person counts the offering and keeps the records of individual contributors, or the same person counts the offering and writes the checks, too.

Once the church accounts are audited, it makes sense to keep the internal controls and the financial records in top shape. It is an important part of the church accounting system.

Unless the account is audited, it will not be acceptable in the business community; it should not be acceptable in the church.

FINALLY

Go through all of that and you have really told the members how it is with their church. Responsible stewardship requires that they be told. And I am convinced that an informed membership will be a responsive membership. The results are bound to mean more dollars in the coffers of your church treasury.

CHAPTER SEVEN

Making Money by Spending Less

Efficient church business management doesn't just happen. It is planned.

Begin reading this chapter with that premise and you will soon learn how planning ought to be done, at least in the area of purchasing, to maximize the utilization of the resources of your church. Unless planning is a significant part of the total operation of your church, you already know how inefficient things are–and expensive–around your place. Without adequate planning, systems and controls, you simply cannot hope to avoid deficit spending, let alone make your budget balance. Do things right, and you can extend the resources of your church even beyond expected limits.

But this book is not a manual on church administration. It's supposed to be a book on ways to improve the financial resources of your church; that is, how to get more money for your church, not how to spend more. At least that is what the previous six chapters have been at pains to say. These last two chapters, on the other hand, deal with spending and how to cut costs (and thus save money) by better spending.

A book on church administration would say what I am about to say now, only in much more detail than is possible in these few pages. If you are looking for a book like that, check the bibliography. Such books are listed there.

PURCHASING PROCEDURES

As I see it, the first step in maximizing resources is to get your purchasing procedures organized. It is the only way you will get "the right thing, of the right quality, in the right quantity, at the right time, at the right place, from the right vendor . . ."* It is the way to make sure you are not paying more than you should for goods and services.

If you choose to make your own personal spending haphazard and unorganized, that is your business. But when you are responsible for the church's money, you have a stewardship responsibility that cannot be ignored. You cannot buy haphazardly. At the minimum, then, the objective of church spending is to get the best buy. And that can only be determined, in large part, by the processes you use to go about doing that spending.

*From *The Art of Purchasing,* by A. L. Macmillan. Copyright © 1959 by A. L. Macmillan. Reprinted by permission of Exposition Press, Inc., Jericho, N.Y. 11753.

A system for buying, or spending church monies, may be nothing more than the back side of a used number 10 envelope in the hip pocket of the pastor. Or it may be an elaborate system of signatures and countersignatures, computers and calculators, salesmen and agents, endless reams of forms and counterforms. In between those extremes will be the happy medium that offers the most efficient, least complicated, most effective purchasing procedure.

The system you use in your church must obviously be useful to you. There is not much point in picking the forms out of someone else's procedures if they don't match your needs. A rather small congregation probably drops all its spending in the pastor's lap. He orders, buys and receives everything the church needs. He is the purchasing agent. Buying is centralized in his office. He is the control. And that is not an all-bad situation. It depends. At least the system that way is bound to be simple.

Yet someone else really ought to do all that, so the pastor can do what he is trained to do—preach, teach, counsel and visit. But out of necessity and convenience, too, at least in the small church, the pastor serving also as purchasing agent may well be the way things can be handled most efficiently. It may be the system by which that church actually saves the most money, too.

When someone is employed and paid a salary, however, or if he is a steady volunteer, then a shift of responsibility from pastor to helper for the minutia of purchasing procedures is appropriate. And in larger churches, a full-time church business administrator is the logical key person in a spending controls system.

The point is, the first point, that some one person must be assigned the responsibility for buying. At least that is going to be necessary if you expect to create the greatest efficiency in your church operations and avoid spending money you may not have to spend. If it is the pastor who must shoulder that responsibility, okay. But purchasing, centralized, is the most efficient way to control spending.

For example, if every teacher in the church school has the authority to go out and buy crayons as the class needs them, money is being thrown away, literally. It is much more efficient to buy all those crayons in quantity and then distribute them as needed. It will most certainly cost less that way, and yet every teacher will still have all the crayons needed. But it will take a system and a procedure to make it work.

Of course, a system just for crayons would be stupid. However, central purchasing works well with almost any supply—paper, tape, janitorial supplies, etc. With one person in charge who knows what everyone needs, duplication is avoided, quantity discounts become possible, and standardization is achieved. It is a process that requires planning, but in the end is almost guaranteed to make more money for your church because you will simply be spending less.

So the system begins by selecting the person to be responsible for purchasing. The options are obvious—from pastor, to the church secretary, a purchasing agent, a business administrator or any interested person. But one person is best. Call that person the purchasing agent.

RESPONSIBILITIES OF THE PURCHASING AGENT*

1. Anticipate the needs of users of materials within the church family.

2. Standardize and simplify products used by various programs of the church.

---

*From the book *Church Purchasing Procedures* by Julian Feldman. Page 20. Copyright © 1964 by Prentice-Hall, Inc. Published by Prentice-Hall, Inc., Englewood Cliffs, N.J.

3. Maintain continuity of supply.

4. Maintain a minimum investment in inventory, consistent with safety and continuity of operations as well as with budgetary objectives. Any overinvestment in inventory is translated ultimately into curtailment of program objectives of the church.

5. Avoid duplication, waste and obsolescence.

6. Maintain standards of quality of materials, based on suitability of use.

7. Procure items at the lowest cost, consistent with safety and economic advantage.

8. Ascertain what equipment and supplies have been declared surplus by any church department; move such surplus supplies and equipment from one department to another where maximum use can be made of them, or dispose of this material to the maximum advantage of the church.

Next, agree on the logical steps that the purchasing agent will follow in buying for the church.

ELEMENTS OF THE PURCHASING PROCEDURE*

1. Ascertainment of need: the decision by someone that something is needed.

2. Statement of the character or quality of the item needed.

3. Statement of the amount of the article or service desired.

4. Determination of when the item is needed.

5. Transmission of the purchase request from the person or department needing it to the person who is responsible for acquiring it.

---

*Julian Feldman, *Church Purchasing Procedures,* p. 21.

6. Consolidation, where possible, of requests from various using departments.

7. Seeking out possible vendors, evaluating them, and negotiating with them for acquisition of the goods.

8. Determination of routing and delivery instructions.

9. Analysis of proposals, final selection of the vendor and placement of the order.

10. Following up on the order to insure shipment in adequate time for most effective use.

11. Receiving the item and checking the invoice.

12. Inspecting the goods.

13. Completion of the record and certification for payment.

14. Payment for the goods.

15. Storage of the goods received.

16. Inventory of the items procured.

17. Research into the way the items are used to determine the effectiveness of the purchasing activity.

And there you have it in a nutshell—what it takes to buy for the church.

Now you need to put all that theory to practice. The purchasing procedure begins in earnest as needs are listed. Obviously purchasing in your church has been going on since before the doors were opened for the first service. But now, with a system, or at least someone in charge, purchasing will continue to meet the needs of all those in the church who use it and utilize its services and facilities, who need something bought to do their jobs better.

Needs vary, of course, and your new purchasing agent will need to sort out appropriate needs. Some needs are more urgent than others. Some will be suggested by the purchasing agent personally, others by the users. But the needs determine what may or may not be purchased.

So when a teacher needs crayons, that need requires a

purchase. When the inventory of janitorial supplies dwindles, a need for more requires a purchase. When salesmen offer ideas for buffing the floors differently at less cost and effort and time, a commitment may be made to purchase a new and larger floor buffer. New programs may require new equipment or supplies. And professional magazines always offer an abundance of new ideas. Some of those ideas may even prove useful for the church. A decision to buy means yet another purchase. Whatever the need, if it is to be fulfilled, it requires a purchase.

Efficient purchasing systems require the use of a purchase requisition. The teacher who needs those crayons, and the custodian whose inventory of wax is low, know their needs and say so on a purchase requisition form. They specify quantity, quality, date needed and any other requirements, including suggested price and source. The purchasing agent, using all the resources available to him, makes a final selection to meet those requirements as closely as possible.

It is not the responsibility of the purchasing agent to tell the teacher whether or not crayons should be used for instruction. That is the teacher's choice. But the purchasing agent can suggest modifications to the specifications in order to get the best price for the best quality. Consolidating the needs for crayons of several teachers into one order offers the possibility of a quantity discount. But every teacher then has to use the same kind of crayons. The purchasing agent attempts to coordinate the order and get the best possible price.

Whatever kind of purchase requisition you agree upon, keep it simple (one copy should be sufficient) and easy to use. Even oral requisitions are not out of order in the small church. The point is, needs must be expressed; and when they are in writing the possibility for confusion or misunderstanding is drastically reduced. The purchasing agent is there to help using departments get what they need. The system should make it possible, therefore, for users to get what they need when they need it at the least possible cost to the church.

THE RIGHT QUANTITY

That cost to the church depends upon a number of factors, including quantity and quality. How much is enough? A fifty-five barrel drum of floor wax will obviously cost less per pound than a ten-pound can, but a church may never use that much wax in twenty years. Besides, the quality of floor wax may be vastly improved within the next few years. Or the church floor may even be refinished so that wax will not be needed any longer.

So, how much is enough? That is the hard question. Yet upon its answer hinges the effectiveness of the purchasing agent. Money can be made (saved) by buying the right quantity at the right time.

These factors must be considered: A small order always costs more per item than a larger order. But the "always buy large" syndrome is wasteful and costly. If the cash resources of the church are limited, it seldom makes sense to borrow to buy to get a larger discount for quantity. (It does pay, however, to borrow to take advantage of a 2/10, net 30 cash discount.) On the other hand, hand-to-mouth buying is inefficient. Picking up a ream of paper or a box of paper clips every time you mimeograph or clip paper together is grossly inefficient and costly. A larger order will not only save money, it will save time and effort, too.

Too many large orders, though, create storage problems; and that costs money. You can figure it out yourself. Storage space may be used more efficiently for some things than for others. Besides, just creating more storage space costs more money, too—for painting, cleaning, lighting, heating and maintenance of the space. There is a happy medium somewhere between hand-to-mouth and carload purchasing for the church. The trick is for your purchasing agent to find that happy point. That is what you have him on the payroll to do.

Furthermore, the costs for processing an order need consideration, too. It is obviously more expensive to buy paper twenty times a year than only once. Aside from the obvious money savings in a large order, you have saved a lot of time, too. And time saved is money in the bank when you pay secretaries and purchasing agents to buy that paper. One order can be processed, normally, in one-twentieth of the time that twenty orders can be processed. Figuring the time of these employees, that could be a substantial saving.

Where small orders are consistently made anyway, one solution is to create a petty cash system. That eliminates a lot of time in writing up orders and generally simplifies the buying process. A small fund is appropriate in the church office. One check replenishes the fund as needed.

The size of a purchase is limited by other factors besides the cost of storage or the cost of writing orders. The quantity of stocks already on hand is important. There is no point in buying six gross of crayons if there are already two gross on hand and only four gross will be used within a reasonable time. An emergency supply of most inventory items is important to maintain, but a larger order just for the sake of a quantity discount may not be best at the time. It all depends.

Furthermore, you need to know how often and when the item will be used. Crayons stored in a hot closet during the summer won't be much good for fall. Special felt pens to be used only once for posters don't need to be the largest size possible. Smaller ones will do, especially since those pens tend to dry out rather fast when the tops are left off. A small order is sometimes more economical than a large one.

Packaging practices may also determine the quantity you buy. You may need only two altar candles, and you may be able to buy them that way. But candles usually are sold twelve to the box. So your best price will be by the dozen. You can buy mimeograph or typing paper in packs of 100 sheets, but a ream is less expensive and certainly the economical way to buy.

Obsolescence and deterioration mean that it makes no sense to buy a ten-year supply of mimeograph paper even if the price break is tremendous. The stuff will yellow and deteriorate in time. You would be lucky to get three years of use out of it all.

And the time it takes to get a product may dictate the quantity you buy. Lead time makes a difference when the teacher wants crayons next week, or the custodian has run dry of wax, or this week's bulletin is due for mimeographing. Lead time is important. Costs can skyrocket when you fail to plan your needs sufficiently far in advance. You may pay twice as much for those crayons or wax or paper if you have to make a sudden dash for the corner five-and-dime instead of planning ahead and buying in quantity from a less expensive place.

For maximum money-use efficiency, follow these guidelines for deciding quantity and time of purchases for your church.*

1. Prepare a realistic yardstick for the minimum ordering quantity for any given class of commodity based on: rate of use, stocks on hand, availability and costs of storage, commercially available quantities and packaging units, ad-

---

*Julian Feldman, *Church Purchasing Procedures,* p. 58.

ministrative costs of processing orders, lead time, deterioration and obsolescence.

2. Consolidate the requirements of all the using departments for the same items in order to increase volume.

3. Purchase materials, as far as possible, in standard package and commercial lots.

4. Make purchases large enough to take advantage of quantity discounts, including all foreseeable needs on an annual basis or longer, where possible, but order no more than is necessary to obtain these price advantages for the designated operating period.

5. Use a blanket supply agreement or requirements contract wherever feasible to purchase items used in repetitive quantities on a regular basis.

THE RIGHT QUALITY

Once you have quantity set at a reasonable limit, quality becomes a factor, too. And that is a bit more difficult to decide. Quality is not limited to same-use identifiable items. You cannot quantify quality, so it becomes harder to define.

All kinds of factors, therefore, go into deciding quality–durability, versatility, efficiency in operation, ease and simplicity of repairs, productivity, convenience to service departments, dependability, etc. Quality purchasing is obviously far more difficult than quantity purchasing. But the right selection of value can make a tremendous difference on costs (initially and long-term), and thus is as important as quantity in keeping costs down.

In selecting quality, price is of course important. But a product is not chosen only on the basis of its low price. Unless the product is useful, no matter how inexpensive, it does not make much sense to buy it, now, does it? At the other extreme, buying quality far in excess of needs is wasteful, too. Quality includes suitability to the needs to be satisfied. If it is not suitable—that is, if its quality is not adequate—any price, no matter how low, is too expensive and a waste.

Of course, the product selected to do the job must be of acceptable quality. And between two products of equal quality, price is important. But the test for suitability is first, price second. The best value is simply the right combination of quality and price.

The right quality, though, may not be the same for everyone. So, who decides what is best? Well, that takes a bit of tactful skill on the part of users, purchasing agent and anyone else involved. The purchasing agent, per se, does not decide, although his opinion should carry tremendous weight. Nor does the user alone decide. In the long run the budget may be the actual deciding factor. Since there can still be honest differences of opinion on quality, there is no pat solution to the dilemma. It is important that there be an awareness by all concerned that personal opinion, likes, dislikes, experiences, relationships and a whole host of other judgments enter into any decision on quality.

Even describing the right quality may be difficult, although purchase requisitions should list specifications for the product. Quality can be designated by brand name or a catalog designation. Or a specific description on the purchase order is appropriate, though difficult. A blueprint or drawing is a very graphic description of the product. Government or trade association standards are useful in setting quality standards. An actual sample of the material can be a rather precise description of quality. Type, size, color, shape or a combination of these various descriptive techniques are all ways to set quality standards in a purchase requisition.

A purchase requisition (or order) can be as specific as

you can or want to make it. Certainly a casual reference to "high" or "acceptable" quality is not enough. What is high or acceptable? So, the requisition must be more specific. What is the composition or makeup of the product? What measurements, weights, sizes are needed? Are there performance specifications? What method of manufacture is preferred? Is some standard specification acceptable?

You see, if you want to get the most for your purchasing dollar, you have to be as specific as you can about what you want. The quality you get depends on it. Of course, you won't go into all this much detail on many items, but so many factors influence quality that you will do well to consider as many as possible before you make a choice.

One of the best ways to satisfy yourself on quality, even if a warranty guarantees all kinds of protection, is to examine the product personally. That way you will know that you are getting what you want, not just what you think you ordered.

THE RIGHT PRICE

Price obviously plays a big part in any purchase. You may have decided on quantity and quality, but if the price is not right, you won't buy. The price you are willing to pay is determined by the value of the product to your church. A new car radiator is of no value to the church that doesn't even own a car. Even the lowest, most ridiculous price on the finest quality radiator, therefore, wouldn't make the church buy. A new lawnmower, however, does have value to the church if it has no mower and its lawn needs mowing. Thus the price the church is willing to pay will depend in part on the urgency for getting the lawn mowed, assuming quality has been agreed upon.

So, what is a proper price? Well, from the point of view of the church, the best price is always the least price possible for the quality and quantity agreed on. It must be fair and reasonable, to be sure, from the point of view of the church; but it must be fair and reasonable for the seller, too, or he won't sell. As in any buy-sell agreement, a meeting of the minds is necessary for a transaction to take place.

Yet, no matter what the price asked and no matter its reasonableness, if the church cannot afford that price, it cannot buy. Thus the purchasing agent must not only consider the best price, but the allocation made by the church's budget as well.

All of which is to say that the market price is really what determines the price paid anyway. No matter how high the price for an item seems, if that is what others are willing to pay, then that will be what the church must also pay if it wants the item. The market is not concerned by what the church can afford to pay or is willing to pay.

The market price is not set at the whim of manufacturers or storeowners, but through a combination of forces in the market: supply, demand and competition. In our free enterprise system, these forces tend to set the price sellers will accept and buyers will pay. At least so long as there are no artificial controls set by governments, there is a price that can be negotiated in a narrow range between bid and asked prices.

And the church is subject to the variations in market price. As demand goes up for fuel oil, the church, along with other users, simply must pay more. As supplies shrink for paper, the church must also pay more. But when lawnmowers are still sitting on the dealer's shelves in November, the price goes down because nobody wants lawnmowers in the winter season. This is a good time for the church purchasing agent to look around for a bargain. After all, next summer the grass will grow again; and if you don't have a mower now, you will need to buy one then. If the quality is right, that lower price may also be right.

The church must buy its goods and services in competition with everyone else. It can hardly expect to influence the market very much; the price it pays will be much the same as others pay. Sometimes, however, discounts are available, not only to churches, but to other purchasers as well. And no matter the name or source of that discount, if it is available to your church, take it.

Discounts come in a variety of sizes. There are quantity discounts for large purchases. It obviously costs less per ream to sell 100 reams as one purchase. The paperwork is reduced, administrative costs are less, transportation less, and so forth. But, as noted before, there is a limit on the quantity of a particular item that the church can use. Yet such discounts are important to the church.

There are also trade discounts. Many suppliers offer such discounts to their customers whom they consider particularly valuable and desirable. Whenever trade discounts or church discounts are offered to your church, there is no reason not to take them. They are all part of the pricing system, and there is just no reason to turn them down. Of course, acceptance of such discounts should in no way obligate the church for special benefits to individuals or organizations.

And there are cash discounts. These offer the prudent purchasing agent an excellent opportunity to make more money for the church. Like all other purchasers, churches are offered the chance to pay less for merchandise by paying their bills more quickly. For the supplier a cash discount is an inducement to get cash quicker. For the customer it is an inducement to pay sooner and to pay less. As a matter of fact, it is usually less expensive to borrow money to pay bills and thus take the discounts, than to miss the discount altogether. Cash discounts are a help, therefore, to both suppliers and customers.

The typical cash discounts offer 2 percent off the invoice price providing payment is made within ten days. In any event, normally, the full payment is due within thirty days. To churches that fail to take cash discounts, it is simply a waste of money that could have gone for programming. The church's stewardship commitment demands that all discounts, especially cash discounts, be taken.

THE RIGHT SOURCE

And finally, in purchasing value, it is important to select good sources. Quality, quantity and price may all be good at one source, but this source may be wrong. Availability, service, continuity of sales and other considerations may make the difference on the source selected for a product. Quality and price may be excellent across town, but when the store down on the corner has the same item, even at a higher cost, accessibility and patronage of a local business may determine the source for an item.

Selection of a supplier is as important in cutting costs as is comparing prices on an item of acceptable quality. Here is what you may want to look for when you are considering the selection of new vendors.

—Is the price right? Are his goods and services available at fair and reasonable prices?

—Is the quality good? Do this supplier's goods and services meet your church's standards? Is quality consistent for all the items you want?

—What about capacity to meet your needs? Does he have adequate facilities, knowledge, capabilities and stock inventory to provide needed service or followup after goods have been bought?

–Check out the management. Is the organization competent and well managed? Is it interested in your church? Is the management progressive, innovative, in tune with the needs of customers? Does the management understand that its own needs are often best served by meeting the needs of your church fully?

–Accessibility? How convenient is the new vendor to your church? Can he furnish what you need when you need it?

–What about his reputation? Is it good? Are his relationships good with the community and his employees? Can he provide evidence of satisfied customers?

WHEN YOU BUY

So, your supplier is selected; quantity, quality and price are determined; and you are ready to buy. If the item is large enough, you may want to do some competitive bidding. Several suppliers may quote their price without knowing what anyone else is quoting. You agree to accept the lowest bid. Bidding may be formal or informal, but it is always best done in writing.

Most of your buying, however, will be done without formal bidding. You and your supplier will agree on a price, either by negotiation or according to the catalog price. You may shop around first, in which case you are really getting quotes from several suppliers. But no matter how you do it, a systematic procedure for buying the right merchandise at the right price at the right time is the purchasing agent's goal. With a listing of qualified suppliers, a "fair and equitable" price can be achieved. This is another way of getting more money in the bank for your church.

TAXES FOR CHURCHES

Your church can save money, too, by not paying taxes.

Hold it! I mean not paying taxes it doesn't owe. There are some taxes a church has no choice but to pay. For other taxes, though, the church can decide whether or not it wants to pay. When it decides to go ahead, then it is obligated to pay the tax. Still, you may be paying taxes you don't owe, or there may be ways to avoid (legally) taxes your church is now paying. Obviously, when you don't pay the taxes you don't owe, you have made money for your church.

For example, in many states church buildings and parsonages are not subject to local real estate taxes. Where such property is exempt, your church may have to make a formal request for exemption; it may not be automatic. Once an exemption is approved, it may not be retroactive if you have gone past any tax periods before filing. If exemptions are available, you can save a lot of money for your church by avoiding taxes on the church properties. Check with your county treasurer where you live for a ruling on the matter.

Church-owned real estate that is used to generate income, however, may be taxable. Parking lots, rental houses and camps rented to others may all be taxable. But it will pay you to file for an exemption anyway. Some loophole might exempt a property even though you thought it was taxable.

Churches are generally exempt from paying local or state sales taxes. You may need to file an exemption certificate with all your vendors to get this exemption, but over the years it will certainly let you pay less than other customers for the same goods. Even the crayons your teacher buys for use in Sunday school may be tax-exempt. Be sure your staff is informed. (Of course, with a central purchasing agent, the problem is easily resolved.)

Churches are not subject to income taxes either, at least not for income received to support the program of the church.

Unrelated business income, however, such as that from a downtown parking lot or a business venture, may be taxable. Where there are such peripheral money-making activities, a church should get competent legal advice on their taxability. Income from bazaar sales, turkey dinners and theatrical activities, even when an admission is charged, is usually exempt. But when churches engage in competitive commercial activities to raise money, they should be prepared to pay a tax, if levied, the same as any commercial enterprise engaged in the same activity has to do. The church, at least in my opinion, should not take advantage of its tax-free status to engage in money-raising activities clearly competitive with the bakery, the restaurant and the dime store just down the street.

A church may or may not be required to pay social security taxes. If the employees request coverage and the church agrees, it is then forever required to comply. (Even the minister may now have his social security and income taxes withheld if he so elects.) Church employees who are covered by social security come under the same social security rules as any other employee. The church is likewise subject to the rules for all employers.

There are ways to keep the church's portion of social security taxes to a minimum, however. For example, social security taxes do not have to be withheld or paid on sick pay. If an employee is absent from work due to illness, no social security tax need be withheld or paid for wages earned during that time. Also, certain categories of agricultural workers are not covered by social security. And of course after an employee earns the maximum annual wage ($13,200 presently), no more tax is withheld or paid. By limiting overtime pay and exercising care in adding employees to the payroll, a church can reduce its social security tax by a few dollars anyway.

The payment of unemployment and workmen's compensation taxes by the church is required in some states. An exemption, however, means dollars saved. Check with your attorney to be sure your church is in compliance with the law. Don't pay taxes you don't owe, but don't evade paying the taxes you do owe.

INSURANCE FOR CHURCHES

Insurance for churches comes in all shapes and sizes, to the detriment of the uninitiated church council person attempting to evaluate what is best for the church. For most of us, the whole business of insurance often leaves us out on the edge. It is difficult to make intelligent decisions because we do not understand the terminology, the limitations, the conditions or even the risks involved.

It is beyond the scope of this book to really clarify the issues, as desperately as that may be needed. Perhaps a few pointers, however, may offer some help in what you can look for and what you may want to avoid. Insurance is a place in which the church can lose a lot of money: by paying too high premiums for coverage it may never use; or by sustaining a dramatic loss because a cheap insurance policy simply did not cover it all.

Fortunately, many denominational headquarters are offering help, if not outright group coverage. This is particularly true for fidelity coverage, and may be extended to fire protection as well. Before your church buys more insurance or when you prepare to evaluate your existing coverage, an inquiry to your church denominational executives may be worthwhile. You may discover that your church is already covered in some areas or that the same coverage is available at much less cost through a church denominational group plan. At least it is worth a ten-cent stamp to find out.

There can be a huge amount of money paid out in insurance premiums. You can stretch your church budget all out of proportion by buying too much insurance, or at least more than you reasonably need or can afford. Actually, if your church has something that needs insuring—a prized painting, teenagers on a camping trip, a stained-glass window during remodeling construction, the life of your minister—you can probably get insurance for it. Maybe you have, but at a price. In fact, if you are willing to pay the premiums, there is almost nothing that you can't buy insurance for. But just because it is available does not necessarily mean that the church ought to have it.

No congregation can possibly afford to take out insurance against every possible hazard that might come at it. You must pick and choose among those insurance coverages that offer the most protection against the greatest hazards at the least cost. The question is not whether insurance is necessary or available. The question is which coverage to pick: what can the church afford? How can its insurance premium dollar be stretched to do the greatest good?

Every church carries insurance of some kind, or at least it ought to. For no matter how careful you are, no matter what safeguards and precautions you take, you simply cannot eliminate the possibility of fire or other catastrophe. Insurance is not purchased in order to make money or collect a bundle when there is a loss. It is bought to provide security against disastrous financial loss. If the church goes up in smoke, with insurance there will at least be some funds to replace and rebuild. Insurance, no matter what the premium cost, is a guarantee that at least some money will be available to rebuild and regroup. For congregational leaders, insurance can be a comforting reassurance.

Fire is the basic coverage, offered along with the other coverages that go with the typical policy. Fire insurance normally covers the contents of a building as well as the building. Where coinsurance clauses are applicable, it is important that you keep your coverage sufficiently high (related to value) to guarantee full payment for any loss.

Obviously fires are not the only perils facing a church building and other church properties. There are many other risks as well. Thus, liability insurance protects against judgments resulting from suits filed against the church. Such coverage provides cost reimbursement just to defend the church even if there is no fault. Thus, such insurance can save the church from burdensome litigation costs as well as actual judgments no matter what the outcome of the suit.

Fire, windstorm, explosion and liability are primary coverages. Anything else is really extra. So whatever else you need depends upon your circumstances. You need to make a careful analysis of your situation to determine what you really need. For this analysis, you will find the services of an insurance appraiser particularly helpful. A survey by an expert, who does not also sell insurance, will outline for you the various types of coverages you ought to carry. You really cannot tell too much about the adequacy of your coverage and the dollar value of all those premiums you have been paying until an expert goes over it all for you. The cost of that survey, done impartially, is well worth the expense.

There is a free booklet available about insurance for churches. Write to the Insurance Information Institute, 110 Williams St., New York, N.Y. 10038. Ask for "A Guide to Property and Casualty Insurance for Churches." There you will find all kinds of helpful hints on glass insurance, boiler insurance, fidelity bonds, church theft insurance, public liability insurance, fire and extended coverages, and so forth.

Insurance coverage is as varied as the hazards; so are the costs. But you need the coverage, and your church budget must anticipate the cost. After all, insurance is good only before a loss. After the fact is too late.

CHAPTER EIGHT

How to Pay Your Pastor More and Balance the Budget, Too

What does a church do to maximize the dollars it spends on its ministers? How does it go about allocating its resources to provide adequate compensation and benefits without putting itself out of business, financially, in the process?

Well, there are ways, believe me, in which the dollars of the church can be stretched farther than you would think possible and still provide substantial benefits for the pastor. You can actually make your pastor's compensation package larger without costing your church anything more, or at the most, not very much more.

Do that and you will be doing your pastor a favor, a favor that will be paid back many times over. And you can do it at hardly any more cost to the congregation than now.

How? It is all a matter of knowing what to do, of taking advantage of the income tax laws, and of putting together a sensible package that helps both pastor and congregation.

Now a pastor's pay package consists of many things, or at least it can. In addition to the obvious base salary, there can be a housing allowance, pension-plan contributions, social security payments, car allowances, health insurance plans, vacations, continuing education, professional expenses and anything else you may wish to provide. Put it altogether and it can be an impressive package. And it will cost money.

Needless to say, unless a congregation is prepared to spend money for a pastor it may as well forget about having one. Ministers come more expensive every year. And congregations seldom step down in the salary for a new pastor. Traditionally costs can only go up. A change of pastors may accelerate the jump, but the cost of ministry, like the cost of most everything else, simply never goes down. It goes up, or at least it ought to go up.

Consider, for example, what may happen if your church fails to up the ante annually and insists it cannot afford to pay any more. When a church forces its pastor to stay at a dishonestly low pay, it harms the pastor and it hurts itself.

Among other things, you will soon discover that your pastor is constantly frustrated in his efforts to get ahead financially, if the pay is too low. A pastor's children do not have the same advantages as other children may. Piano lessons, dancing, even the frivolities of popcorn and coke at a ballgame, not to mention orthodontists, opticians and college costs, may simply be unavailable.

If you could look through my files, you would see letter after letter citing all the things a pastor cannot do because he simply doesn't have the money to do it with, things that many members may take for granted.

And all this is particularly true when you put that pastor down in the middle of an upper-class suburban community, in an expensive parsonage, yet fail to keep the pay high enough to meet the expectations (and the costs) of that community. It is a frightening and a frustrating experience, no less for the pastor than for his wife and children.

A pastor has enough problems to cope with day after day. Certainly a congregation, your congregation, ought to make sure the pastor's pay is high enough to meet the needs and expectations of your community.

Low-paid pastors usually have a very negative attitude toward the church, and they feel guilty about that attitude. Having committed themselves to the task of shepherding people in the way of the Gospel, they prefer not to be negative. They want to support that church. But when they are taken advantage of, they do begin to rebel, at least inwardly, seething at the injustice of it all. And of course, it isn't fair.

Solutions would come in part by boosting pay. But unilateral upward adjustments, though welcome, obviously will not necessarily be received with open arms. A bit of negotiating and discussion is needed about what that adjustment ought to be, not only from the congregation's point of view, but from the pastor's point of view as well. Even pastors should have the privilege of suggesting what is fair and equitable. The congregation sets the final amounts, to be sure—the congregation and not the chairman of the finance committee. But a pastor's concern should be considered.

Offer your pastor an opportunity to discuss his pay with you. Then set the amount within reasonable limits and you have taken a long step toward easing the tension and hostile attitude to which low-paid preachers are susceptible.

Furthermore, low-paid pastors cannot respond to community responsibilities the way they want to. They simply cannot afford to give to the United Appeals or join the Rotary, even if they want to. Pleas for contributions to local civic causes go ignored. And support for a cause, as noble as it may be, is only half-hearted, if anything at all, because pastors who cannot put their money on the barrelhead are not likely to speak out publicly on the issues they want to be in favor of.

Nor will a pastor's family be involved in community affairs, either. If both spouses must work to help stave off bill collectors, there is no time for the PTA and the Little League and the Girl Scouts. You not only do your pastor a disservice by paying too little, you also deprive your community of exceptional leadership that it may desperately need.

Any pastor receiving low pay will be tempted to find more money somewhere, somehow. That means some pastors moonlight, with or without the permission of the church. Either way, the moonlighting cuts into the ministry to the church. When a pastor must earn money doing something else because his pay is such a piddling amount, it is the church that ends up on the short end of the deal. The church expects a full-time job to be done (and that is more than any forty hours a week!); yet they won't get it, nor can they get it, if their pastor is holding down another job, too.

Now, so-called tent-making ministries are a moonlighting situation, but intentionally so. By agreement the church says it can only afford a part-time minister, so it expects the pastor to do some other work as well. "We'll pay less and we'll expect only a proportionate share of time." And all that is quite proper. It is planned that way.

But when a pastor has a full-time job as minister of a church, the pay should be appropriate for the job, not something less. And a pastor's working hours, then, should be for that church; he is not being forced to do something else because the church does not pay enough. Moonlighting, serious moonlighting in an extensive way by your pastor, will damage your church far more than you realize. To let those conditions exist means you are getting even less for your dollars than you think. It is a poor policy of resource allocation. It will cost you money in the long run.

Of course, the place where low pay really hits the pastor hardest is in retirement. Since benefits of most retirement plans are based on contributions to the plan and contributions are based on salary, low-paid ministers get low pensions. Even social security works that way, although there are minimum pensions regardless of dollars contributed. Nevertheless, when your church pays a low salary, it also "pays" a low retirement income, too.

And if a minister can't afford to retire because his retirement pay won't be enough, because contributions have been so low because pay has been meager, that pastor won't quit when he should at age 65 or 70 or even 75. He can't afford to. Obviously, the church will be hurt by that.

Older ministers who cannot afford to retire, yet who want to retire, know they are a burden to the church, but they can't really do anything about it. It's too late. All of which means it will cost your church more money if you do not pay enough now. Low pay is simply not good resource allocation, not in the long run. Besides, it is immoral to start with.

There is also a tendency among low-paid pastors to leave the ministry simply because they can't afford to stay in any longer. Other jobs pay better, so that is where they go. And that too costs the church more money. Maybe that cost will not show up directly on your monthly financial statement, but again it may. It costs money to train pastors, and your benevolence dollars are used to support the seminaries in which they are trained. Let the pastors leave the ranks after the church has spent all that money to train them for a job, and it will cost your church money. It means more benevolence dollars to train someone else.

But even the cost to the person who leaves the ministry may be dreadful, too—cost in retraining dollars, defeatism, frustration. Pay them enough, and most pastors will stick it out because that is what they want to do and that is what they are trained to do.

If you have ever tried to recruit someone for a job that pays less than the prevailing wage rate, you have some idea of what it takes to recruit new students for seminaries. Frankly, no one goes into the ministry because he or she expects to get rich from the job. Some do get paid far more than others, but the vast majority of pastors receive enough to meet their commitments and to enjoy life as most other people do. Does yours?

Every pastor I know expects to be paid a fair wage. Yet when stories abound about how bad off some ministers are, young, energetic, talented men and women are going to think twice before jumping onto that bandwagon. They may not have visions of wealth, but they certainly expect a reasonable compensation. Unless they can be convinced that it will be so, recruitment for the ministry will be extremely difficult.

All of which doesn't paint a very pleasant picture of the ministry for the community. In fact, the traditional image of the pastor is a person of low pay. So ministers receive discounts at department stores, get professional no-charge service from physicians and dentists and enjoy other similar prerogatives in the community. And all because it is assumed or known that the pastor is paid very little and thus needs some help to make it. What do you suppose that does to a pastor's self-respect?

Until pastors are paid enough—and we will find out in a moment how "enough" can be arranged—they will be a drag on society or at least will give that impression. The image has not always been good to the person on the street.

So what does a church do? Pay more? Perhaps. Or at least it will take the time to examine carefully just what all goes into that pay package to see if some rearrangement can't improve it all. Sure, the rearrangement may cost the church some money, but figure it out. In the long run it will make more money for your church because you will have a pastor who is giving full energy to your church. That pastor will not be frustrated (at least not with his pay!). His attitudes will be positive, there will not be a need to moonlight, and a reasonable retirement income can be anticipated; your church is likely to be able to keep its pastor for a long time, too, if you want to.

A pastor's low salary is not to be viewed with complacency. Whether you believe it or not, I am convinced that there actually can be more money for your church when you pay your pastor more!

Now, putting that pay package together involves more than just agreeing on a salary and some fringe benefits. To begin with, a distinction needs to be made between what is compensation and what is reimbursement of professional expenses. You are not doing your church or your pastor any favors by lumping everything you pay into one figure and calling that salary. What it costs you to have a pastor and what that pastor's actual compensation is, are two different amounts.

To be reasonable about it, you must admit that the car allowance you pay, for example, is not compensation, by any stretch of the imagination. Your church is paying for the costs of operating an automobile. If the pastor didn't drive a car on church business, there would be no costs and the church wouldn't need to reimburse for anything. But because the pastor is required to drive around, there is an expense, a professional expense. And that expense is a legitimate church cost for having a pastor. Most church leaders would agree.

The point is, though, that it is important to keep the costs and the compensation separate. The same goes for professional books. The church pays for them because that is a legitimate cost of having a pastor. His need for those books is not personal, it is for his congregation. Reimbursements for professional expenses are indeed a cost for having a pastor, but they are not compensation. And the distinction is important.

So what do you put into that package? How do you use the resources available for the cost of ministers to the best advantage? How can you make more money for the church by putting your pastor's pay package together appropriately? Here's how.

Start with compensation that is not reimbursement of professional expenses. That includes base salary, housing, pension contributions paid by the church, health and accident and life insurance premiums paid by the congregation, any social security allowance provided, and other benefits such as vacations, continuing education opportunities, sabbatical leaves and so forth.

And the obvious place to begin with that list, of course, is salary, for that is the largest piece of compensation paid and usually the most important to consider.

There is no way possible for the church to keep cutting costs here and still make money for the church. Ministers will always cost more, at least for one person. A decision on one pastor instead of two may mean less cost, but the basic costs of having a pastor simply require the payment of money. And the amount is important.

You will get the most mileage out of the salary paid if you make it enough to be attractive, yet not frivolous. A comparison with salaries paid to professional persons in the community, not just in the congregation, with similar training and experience will tell you whether you are in the ball park or not. That information should be available from the local chamber of commerce.

How much you advance that pay each year is important, too. You will want to reward a good job done, allow for inflation, and offer something for added responsibilities. Do a bad job in raising your pastor's base pay, and all the other things you have done with that package go down the drain. Just as you like to have some monetary recognition at the place you work for a job well done, for the confidence your employer has in you, so does your pastor appreciate the same kind of consideration. Treat him as a human being with sensitivities just like your own, and you will do wonders for his morale and for the good of the church, too. A generous pay boost is never out of line.

But it is in the supplemental benefits area where you can save money for your church and yet provide additional benefits for your pastor.

For example, take the matter of housing. Now you would think that providing a home would be the one thing your pastor wants and needs from the church. Besides it is a good investment for the church. That is the traditional view. But think again. In the long run—ten, twenty years down the pike—both of you will be farther ahead financially, I am convinced, by having a housing allowance instead of a parsonage. The church pays the minister a full salary, equal to worth, the same as that received by any employee anywhere, designates a part of it as housing allowance for the tax benefit of the pastor, and then lets the minister spend that full salary in any way he wants. Like most employees outside the ministry, he will use a part of it for a home, either purchased or rented.

In that way the church treats the pastor the same as

any employee. It offers the option of finding whatever type of housing the pastor wants and can afford on his own.

Now for income tax purposes the church specifically designates a portion of that salary as housing allowance. To do so permits the pastor to exclude that much from income, providing it is used to "provide a home." Since the minister who lives in a church-owned home does not have to report as income the rental value of that home, ministers without church-owned parsonages may exclude a housing allowance. Thus, in this way, pastors in both situations are treated the same for tax purposes.

The advantage to the minister is clear. The advantage to the church may not be so clear. But the average minister probably enjoys about a $600 to $800 tax break between a parsonage and an allowance. In addition, with his own home, the pastor itemizes deductions and gets yet another tax break for the interest on the mortgage and the real-estate taxes on the house. That could be another $200 to $300 tax break. These tax breaks justify the use of the housing allowance. The homeowner costs, listed as itemized deductions, really provide a double tax break.

Add to the tax advantage the importance of building up equity in a home, and you can see quite clearly that in the long run it is distinctly advantageous to the minister to have an allowance and thus be able to purchase a home. This, of course, says nothing about the advantages or disadvantages of buying a home or how to go about it, but that is the responsibility of the minister and is more appropriately left to a book on personal finance for ministers.*

I believe that the church, like the minister, ends up with an advantage. Aside from the obvious fact of being able to

*From *Making It on a Pastor's Pay,* by Manfred Holck, Jr., Ch. 4. Copyright © 1974 by Abingdon Press.

help the minister enjoy some financial benefits from having an allowance, an allowance does get the church out of the real estate business, eliminates the need for a committee to look after the parsonage property, avoids all the problems associated with maintaining, repairing, replacing and furnishing a parsonage. It simply reduces the responsibility of the church in an area unrelated to the real mission of the church. Besides, over the years, the costs involved in purchasing, financing and maintaining that home may very well balance out to what the church would pay for an allowance anyway. There may be exceptions, to be sure, but I am convinced that it will cost the church no more, certainly less in time and agony over minor decisions on maintenance and repair and new curtains, to provide an allowance than to own the home itself.

Obviously someone who is quick with a pencil can figure out the advantages either way, but if the church counts the security of the pastor as anything, nine times out of ten the church will have more money with an allowance than with its own home.

If your congregation is considering a church parsonage, ask yourself these basic questions: Will the next pastor's family fit this home? Is it reasonably modern? How near is it to the church? Are the women finicky about the curtains and the walls, especially where there are several small children? How about you? Would you prefer to pay rent (as your pastor does in a parsonage) or own your own home, if you had the choice and could afford it? What kind of answers do you get when you raise those questions in your church?

Financially your church may come out even on the matter, either way. But for your pastor don't ignore the significant tax break he or she will get by owning a home. It can mean money in the bank for your pastor to own a home!

Most pastors belong to some kind of pension program. Your pastor should also. And your church should be making regular contributions on behalf of its pastor to the plan. In any pension plan you can save your pastor money by making those contributions directly to the pension plan rather than to him. And it won't cost the church one dime more.

For example, if your pastor's plan calls for a contribution of 4 percent plus 8 percent by the church, a $10,000 salary would require a total contribution of $1,200 a year. If the 4 percent, $400, is paid out of the pastor's paycheck, there will be income tax to pay on the income used to pay the 4 percent. In the 14 percent tax bracket, paying that $400 out of his take-home pay will cost the pastor another $64 (14 percent times $400). But if the church pays that $400, there will be no income tax to be paid on it (until received in retirement.) Reduce the pastor's salary by the $400–if that is what you prefer rather than raising the salary by that much–and it won't cost the church anything more to pay the full 12 percent contribution. But it will save the pastor a beautiful $64 free and clear! Now there is a way to make money for your church, besides boosting the pastor's pay and not paying him any more.

That is so obvious, it's a wonder more congregations don't do it that way.

Much the same savings is possible on health, accident, disability and group life insurance premium costs. The church can pay those costs and thus save money for the pastor, too. For example, if the pastor must pay all those premium costs out of take-home pay, it will cost a minimum 14 percent of the total premium cost plus the premium itself. When the church pays the premium, though, that 14 percent tax is money in the bank for your pastor.

If you have to reduce salary to justify paying those premiums, okay, that's a way to do it. It will still save the pastor a minimum of 14 percent, and it won't be costing the church any more to do it that way. But how much more generous to add that premium cost to the base salary. It will cost the church more, to be sure, but not that much more; and it will certainly be appreciated by the pastor.

The matter of the self-employment social security tax is a constant and increasing concern to your pastor. It is usually difficult enough to make ends meet on a pastor's pay; but when this tax keeps on going up, it really adds an uncontrollable burden. The 1974 tax, which your pastor is required to pay if he earns at least $13,200, is $1,043, up more than 80 percent in the last three years! Of course, the tax is for a good cause and the benefits are still significant, I believe; but 7.9 percent of income going to social security is a burden, don't kid yourself. Most ministers now pay far more social security tax than they do income tax.

Here is a plan that will not necessarily save your church any money, but the congregation can surely do its pastor a service by picking up the tab on that tax for him. By law the church cannot pay the tax itself, but it can certainly offer an allowance equal to the maximum tax that will provide the funds the pastor can use to pay the tax. You won't save any money that way, but you will offer a benefit for whatever long-term advantage that may be to your church program.

Yet, if you do not want to add that allowance as an additional burden to your already out-of-balance church budget, you can, once again, reduce the pastor's salary and offer an equal allowance instead. But then agree to pay the maximum tax in each subsequent year. That way your pastor will not need to worry when the tax goes up next year because the allowance will automatically increase to take care of the added cost. The payment of the increase means a small additional cost to the church each year, but it is certainly a welcome boost to the take-home pay of the pastor. It is another way, at comparatively small cost to the church, to help the pastor stretch his bank account a little bit more.

Needless to say, your church can find many other ways to help your pastor financially at little or no additional cost. Any added boost will always be welcome. And usually the fringe benefits can offer the best financial advantage, because taxes can be reduced that way.

Normally the cost of continuing education is a tax-deductible item for your pastor. But again, if the church assumes that cost, it is a benefit to the pastor. The church may even be able to get discounts unavailable to the pastor, thus saving both some money.

A sabbatical leave offers the opportunity for your pastor to take extended time off at full pay for additional study. Even though it will obviously cost your church some money, it can certainly be a tremendous help to your pastor. Again, down the road, it will also help your church by improving your pastor's competence; and that could get you some more money, too!

Vacations do come in all sizes, and you will want to provide a vacation opportunity for your pastor, too. A full month is appropriate. Your cost? Someone to preach on Sunday, perhaps, unless laymen take over the task, which of course they can do, if they will. That can cut your costs on the pastor's vacation Sundays.

Reimbursement of professional expenses is another matter. As I noted earlier, it is important to make a clear distinction between reimbursements and compensation. And the distinction should be made on the church budget, too, not just in the calculation of the total package.

The most significant reimbursement is, obviously, the car allowance. Now you will really be doing your pastor a favor if you go all the way and provide him with a church-owned car. Cost-wise and tax-wise, too, that is the best break for him. But it is not necessarily the best arrangement for the church. Owning that car has all the same kinds of problems as owning a parsonage. As an alternative, you may be better off to lease. Though leasing, too, has disadvantages, namely the expense.

The most popular method of reimbursement, and probably the least expensive for the church, is a regular car allowance each month. This is really the easiest method all around. At least for the church. No one has to worry about calculating a new monthly payment or whether all the car bills are paid or even if the amount is adequate. The church sets an amount and the pastor is paid those dollars in the same check as his pay. But, you will have to admit, a car allowance is not really a very good way for the pastor.

The costs of operating a car depend to a large extent on the miles driven. Thus $100 a month may cover costs this month; but next month, if twice the miles are driven, it won't. And to say that it all averages out in a year's time is to miss the point entirely. Maybe it does, but not likely. A flat allowance each month is simply not an equitable arrangement. It may be more than is needed to cover costs, in which case it is costing the church money; or it may be insufficient, which is more likely, and is unfair to the pastor because it is costing him money.

The Internal Revenue Service suggests a procedure that is probably most fair to church and pastor alike. For tax purposes, your pastor can deduct 12 cents a mile for the first 15,000 miles he drives his car on church business, and 9 cents for each additional mile. Or he can deduct actual costs, but the mileage arrangement offers the least complicated method. And it is a method that can be coupled very well with a church's mileage reimbursement plan. If the Revenue Service says 12 cents a mile is a reasonable cost for operating a car, on the average, a church should be able to justify the same allowance.

Thus, each month the pastor can report to the church treasurer the number of miles driven. A check to him can be written at the rate of 12 cents a mile. The allowance then is income, but the offsetting deduction cancels out any possible tax. If your pastor has actual operating costs for his car of less than 12 cents a mile, he is ahead financially with some tax-free income—the difference between what you paid him and what he actually spent.

Chances are that that mileage allowance will not cost your church any more than the previous fixed monthly amount; it may even be less. The point is, though, that it will certainly be a very fair way to make sure the pastor is reimbursed for all car expenses incurred and not just part of them.

Your pastor has other professional expenses, too, for which reimbursement should also be made. These are the costs of books, magazines, robes, office supplies, baptismal certificates and all those other costs incurred because of the nature of the job. While these are all deductible on the pastor's tax return, an allowance from the church helps to ease the burden on his pocketbook.

If your church is looking for a sample pay package, here are two arrangements that may be useful.* The first plan has the following items:

1. Salary minimum schedule for senior pastor (80% for associates) assuming 1974 dollars.

*From *Making It on a Pastor's Pay,* by Manfred Holck, Jr., pp. 24-26.

Years of service	Adult members up to 300	300–600	600–900	900–plus
Up to 5 years	$ 8,500	$ 9,000	$ 9,500	$10,000
6 to 10 years	10,000	10,500	11,000	11,500
11 to 15 years	11,500	12,000	12,500	13,000
Over 15 years	13,000	13,500	14,000	14,500

2. Free use of a church-owned home or a housing allowance equal to at least 25 percent of the base salary.

3. Car allowance equal to at least 12 cents a mile.

4. A minimum of 12 percent of salary, housing allowance, and social security allowance paid by the church to a pension plan.

5. An allowance for social security taxes equal to the maximum self-employment social security tax applicable each year.

6. A health and death benefit insurance plan, all premiums to be paid by the church.

7. At least four weeks' vacation.

8. Two additional weeks for continuing education with tuition payment made by the church.

9. A three-month sabbatical for each six years of service with the same church.

10. And, full reimbursement for all professional expenses.

Another plan proposes the following arrangement: Beginning the first year in the ministry, a basic salary of $100 a week is proposed, this salary increasing $5 a week for each year in the ministry. Reimbursement for automobile expenses is set at $35 a week, including the cost of replacement. A provision for various state, federal and social security taxes suggests $35 a week with a $1 per week increase for each year in the ministry.

The pastor is provided with a parsonage and utilities or a housing allowance to cover both (assumed at 25 percent of the base salary). A weekly pension allowance of $15 plus disability insurance coverage is suggested. A book and study-material allowance is also recommended for which $100 a year is anticipated. If your church followed that pattern, the cost to the church would be something like this:

	1st year	10th year	20th year	30th year
Base salary	$ 5,200	$ 7,800	$10,400	$13,000
Automobile allowance	1,820	1,820	1,820	1,820
Tax allowance	1,820	2,340	2,860	3,380
Pension plan	780	1,300	1,820	2,340
Health insurance, etc.	312	468	624	780
Book and study material	100	100	100	100
Parsonage/housing	1,300	1,950	2,600	3,250
Total cost to church	$11,332	$15,778	$20,224	$24,670

However, that would not all be income to the pastor. Here is a schedule showing the real income, fringe benefits and expense reimbursements in this situation. Divided this way, the pastor's net take-home pay would be much less than the total cost for having a pastor.

	1st year	10th year	20th year	30th year
Real income:				
Base salary	$ 5,200	$ 7,800	$10,400	$13,000
Tax allowance	1,820	2,340	2,860	3,380
Parsonage/housing	1,300	1,950	2,600	3,250
Net take-home pay	$ 8,320	$12,090	$15,860	$19,630
Fringe benefits:				
Pension plan	$ 780	$ 1,300	$ 1,820	$ 2,340
Health insurance, etc	312	468	624	780
Book and study material	100	100	100	100
	$ 1,192	$ 1,868	$ 2,544	$ 3,220
Reimbursements:				
Automobile allowance	$ 1,820	$ 1,820	$ 1,820	$ 1,820
Total cost to church	$11,332	$15,778	$20,224	$24,670

It is obvious from all this that the take-home pay and the church expense for having a pastor are not the same thing. This distinction is important.

If you want to know the tax advantages (approximate) for a homeowning pastor compared to those for a pastor living in a parsonage or even compared with your own situation, take a look at this chart:

	Layman who rents	Layman who buys	Clergyman with parsonage	Clergyman who rents	Clergyman who buys
1. Base salary	$10,000	$10,000	$ 7,000	$ 7,000	$ 7,000
2. House allowance	-0-	-0-	-0-	3,000	3,000
3. Income	$10,000	$10,000	$ 7,000	$10,000	$10,000
4. House allowance exclusion	-0-	-0-	-0-	3,000	3,000
5. Income subject to income tax	$10,000	$10,000	$ 7,000	$ 7,000	$ 7,000
6. Exemptions and deductions	3,500	3,500	3,500	3,500	3,500
7. Total	$ 6,000	$ 6,500	$ 3,500	$ 3,500	$ 3,500
8. Interest, taxes	-0-	1,500	-0-	-0-	1,500
9. Taxable income	$ 6,500	$ 5,000	$ 3,500	$ 3,500	$ 2,000
10. Income tax	$ 1,255	$ 910	$ 595	$ 595	$ 310

That is a $285 tax saving for the homeowning clergyman. He pays $945 less income tax than a layman who rents.

Even a social security allowance makes a difference taxwise, as I have mentioned. Check over the following chart to see what difference it makes in take-home pay to your pastor whether or not you offer this allowance:

COMPARISON OF NET TAKE-HOME PAY WITH OR WITHOUT A SOCIAL SECURITY ALLOWANCE

Assume in 1971 a reduction in salary just to get an annual social security allowance started. In subsequent years no other salary increases are received except increase in Social Security allowance to maximum amount.

	1971		1972		1973		1974	
	w/o	w/	w/o	w/	w/o	w/	w/o	w/
1. Salary	$12,000	$11,415	$12,000	$11,415	$12,000	$11,415	$12,000	$11,415
2. Allowance	-0-	585	-0-	675	-0-	864	-0-	1,043
3. Income	12,000	12,000	12,000	12,090	12,000	12,279	12,000	12,458
4. Exemptions and deductions	4,000	4,000	4,000	4,000	4,000	4,000	4,000	4,000
5. Taxable income	8,000	8,000	8,000	8,090	8,000	8,279	8,000	8,458
6. Income tax (estimated)	1,600	1,600	1,600	1,618	1,600	1,650	1,600	1,680

	1971		1972		1973		1974	
	w/o	w/	w/o	w/	w/o	w/	w/o	w/
7. Income after tax	6,400	6,400	6,400	6,472	6,400	6,629	6,400	6,778
8. Social security tax	585	585	675	675	864	864	1,056	1,043
9. Net income	5,815	5,815	5,725	5,797	5,536	5,765	5,344	5,735
10. Exemptions and deductions added back	4,000	4,000	4,000	4,000	4,000	4,000	4,000	4,000
11. Net take-home pay	9,815	9,815	9,725	9,797	9,536	9,765	9,344	9,735
12. Additional take-home pay when allowance provided		-0-		72		229		391

First column in each year is income without an allowance; second column assumes an allowance equal to the maximum social security self-employment tax.

What you pay your pastor is important—to him and to your congregation. How you pay him is important, too. Because how you pay him could make a difference in how much it costs your church and him. Put that compensation package together right and you can save your church some money and boost your pastor's pay besides—which is a combination that's hard to beat!

BIBLIOGRAPHY

BIBLIOGRAPHY

Banker, John C. *Personal Finance for Ministers*. Philadelphia, Pa.: The Westminster Press. 1973.

Bramer, John C. *Efficient Church Business Management*. Philadelphia, Pa.: The Westminster Press. 1960.

Bratgard, Helge. *God's Stewards* (A Theological Study of the Principles and Practices of Stewardship). Minneapolis, Minn.: Augsburg Publishing House. 1963.

Crawford, John R. *A Christian and His Money*. Nashville, Tenn.: Abingdon Press. 1967.

Crist, Richard, ed. *Your Church* (6 times annually). 198 Allendale Road, King of Prussia, Pa.

Crockett, N. David. *Sound Financial Stewardship.* New York: Morehouse-Barlow Co., Inc. 1973.

Ditzen, Lowell R. *Handbook of Church Administration.* New York: Macmillan, Inc. 1962.

Feldman, Julian. *Church Purchasing Procedures.* Englewood Cliffs, N.J.: Prentice-Hall, Inc. 1964.

Gray, Robert N. *Managing the Church* (Business Methods and Church Business Administration). Enid, Okla.: The Phillips University Press. 1971.

Gross, Malvern. *Financial and Accounting Guide for Non-Profit Organizations.* New York: Ronald Press. 1972.

Harrison, George W. *Church Fund Raising.* Englewood Cliffs, N.J.: Prentice-Hall, Inc. 1964.

Hersey, Norman, ed. *Church Management: the Clergy Journal* (10 times annually). 115 N. Main St., Mt. Holly, N.C.

Holck, Manfred. *Accounting Methods for the Small Church.* 2711 N. Limestone, Springfield, Oh. Clergy, Inc. 1974.

______. *Making It on a Pastor's Pay.* Nashville, Tenn.: Abingdon Press. 1974.

______. *Money Management for Ministers.* Minneapolis, Minn.: Augsburg Publishing House. 1966.

______. *Pre-Parish Planner* (Personal Finance for Newly Ordained Ministers). Minneapolis, Minn.: Ministers' Life Resources. 1974.

______. *Tax Planning for the Clergyman.* Englewood Cliffs, N.J.: Prentice-Hall, Inc. 1973.

______. ed. *Church and Clergy Finance* (bi-weekly financial newsletter for ministers) Minneapolis, Minn.: Ministers' Life Resources.

Holt, David R. *Handbook of Church Finance.* New York: Macmillan, Inc. 1960.

Kantonen, T. A. *A Theology of Christian Stewardship.* Philadelphia, Pa.: Muhlenberg Press. 1956.

Kuntz, Kenneth. *Wooden Chalices* (New Ideas for Stewardship). St. Louis, Mo.: The Bethany Press. 1963.

Leach, William, H. *Handbook of Church Management.* Englewood Cliffs, N.J.: Prentice-Hall, Inc. 1958.

McKay, Arthur R. *Servants and Stewards* (The Teaching and Practice of Stewardship). Philadelphia, Pa.: The Geneva Press. 1963.

McMullen, John S. *Stewardship Unlimited.* Richmond, Va.: John Knox Press. 1964.

Page, Harry R. *Church Budget Development.* Englewood Cliffs, N.J.: Prentice-Hall, Inc. 1964.

Peterson, Robert E. *Handling the Church's Money.* St. Louis, Mo.: The Bethany Press. 1965.

Rolston, Holmes. *Stewardship in the New Testament Church.* Richmond, Va.: John Knox Press. 1959.

Scotford, John R.. *When You Build Your Church.* New York: Channel Press, Inc. 1958.

Taylor, Robert C. *How to Maintain Your Church Buildings and Grounds.* Old Tappan, N.J.: Fleming H. Revell Company. 1962.

Thompson, T. K., ed. *Stewardship in Contemporary Theology.* New York: Association Press. 1960.

Twenty Stewardship Sermons. Minneapolis, Minn.: Augsburg Publishing House. 1960.

Walker, Arthur L. *Church Accounting Methods.* Englewood Cliffs, N.J.: Prentice-Hall, Inc. 1964.

Werning, Waldo J. *The Stewardship Call.* St. Louis, Mo.: Concordia Publishing House. 1965.